Wax Night

in

Montana

When women gather to strip away pleasantries,

revealing the beauty and depth of True Friendship

* *

KATIE DAWN

Praise for Wax Night

"The author's voice comes through clearly as feminine, both irreverent and sacred, with the unmistakable Montana DNA of bravery, soul, and grit. After reading Wax Night, I am inspired to erase my own dark corners of bitterness with deep and intentional connection... and self-love. I am left with salt-dry tears and so much gratitude for the depth of vulnerability!"

S.J.

"An entertaining memoir that will have you laughing and crying, as well as connecting with the strength and bond of women."

D.W.

"It was so raw and honest and heartfelt. That was some of the most compelling writing I've ever read."

R.G.

"I was engaged by this story - pulled back in time and time again - by the multiplicity of stories, the pain that informed all but did not define, the hilarity, the sass, the love."

L.S.

"Within the first chapter of Wax Night and on throughout the book I had moments of out loud laughter. If you want to laugh, cry and enjoy a fun heartwarming book, then sit down with a glass of wine and crack it open."

W.C.

CONTENTS

Part Three

Acknowledgements

*I*t does take a village. If not for the encouragement and cheerleading of my dearest friends and family, this book would not be published. If not for them, there would be no story to tell. That said, I need to thank a specific handful directly for their influence, editing, and guidance with this, my debut book:

Moira, my mentor and writing professor, your love for me is so strong, I can feel it halfway around the world. From the bottom of my heart, thank you. Also, my friend, Christine, if it were not for your sage advice to "trust your readers," this book would be meager in comparison to what it is now.

Dr. Donna K. Wallace, spiritual guide and Book Architect extraordinaire, how can I put into words the value of your guidance and companionship, your expertise? The ways in which you led me from dream to deadline, from paper to print, were nothing short of miraculous. I hope our journey together continues long enough for me to prove to you my gratitude.

Members of my family who are not mentioned by name in the pages that follow, I would choose each one of you to be parts of my journey, even if you hadn't been God given. I consider myself blessed with the family into which I was born, wed, and informally adopted.

Friends that molded my childish and younger self, to you I owe a debt. Jill, Sunny, Summer, Hillary, and Oakley, you were instrumental in forming the essence of who I am today: whole, strong, loved. Thank you for friendships that transcend time and space and are daily felt within the threads of my life.

Little Brother, I am immensely proud of you and your accomplishments. I see the incredible man you have grown to be. Big Brother, I am immensely proud of you, too. The fact that you're still standing and successful is a monumental testament to your strength of character. We have all been through a lot together. Thank you for the company along our journey.

Mom, you have left us behind here on earth but live within us and manifest in the strength and compassion with which we strive to live each day. Your memory resides forever in our hearts. We love you immeasurably and miss you with every breath. From each fiber in my being, thank you, Mom.

Dad, you are one of my greatest inspirations. You've taught me more than anyone about the joys of feeling deep emotion, the power of vulnerability, and the riches of belonging. I'm so fortunate to be able to call you my dad. And to your fearless companion, GrandPam, we are so blessed to have you in our lives. You've supported Dad and the rest of our family in ways we may never be able to repay. I've held stories of your support for Book Two so they will shine all the brighter. Granny (Lisa), the same is true for you. Your stories will radiate in pages not yet published.

I cannot measure the overwhelming sense of possibility and wonder my sons have bestowed upon me. They've forever changed my life by adding dimensions of excitement and perspective I could find no other way. To my older son, thank you for the encouragement you give with the pride I see shining in your eyes as we dance in the kitchen. You've been my champion. To my younger son, thank you for the unbridled enthusiasm and effervescence you shower on me daily.

I couldn't have built such a life without the strong, yet gentle, hands and ruggedly tender heart of my husband. You roped my heart and have held it tight for the past seventeen years. Thank you, Babe, for your unwavering support in all things.

Today, I am rich beyond measure because of my family and friendships. In addition to a loyal community, and good men surrounding me, I have many women in my life that help motivate me to chase my dreams. I make a few specific mentions here, some of which have already made the pages of the second book in the series. Thank you to the following for being you and being in my life: Aunt Gini, Bobbi, Chanda, Renee, Lorca, Karen, and Rhonda. I will leave my acknowledgements in the pages hereafter for my Wax Night posse and other motherly, inspiring women who surround me. Each word written is my way of showing appreciation. These women allow me to go to the depths of despair with the knowledge that they will pull me back from it if I'm not strong enough to do so myself. They elevate me with unbridled delight and joy. For these women, my gratitude is immeasurable. This is my way of shouting it from the rooftops.

Preface

*S*ince the moment the first women in the world joined to celebrate community, they've plaited one another's hair, scrubbed virgin brides with herbs and oils, and kept traditions of blessing ways for birthing. Rites of passage were marked with congregations of women offering wisdom, comfort, and solidarity. To marry a young woman was often to marry the tribe. To bring a child into the world meant a celebration of all life and those conduits that brought it forth.

Women have not only gathered together since ancient times to celebrate relationships and such primitive rites but also perfected the arts of cleanliness and fashion in the form of hair removal for many generations. In fact, this practice has been enacted in almost all human cultures since early times. The Mediterranean and Orient have the longest-standing record of hair removal, dating back as far as 4000 B.C. Inhabitants of Greece and Rome, as well as many others, considered this way of maintaining themselves a means of distinction, proper hygiene, and religious acumen.

Many cultures in ancient times used pumice stones and seashell razors to achieve smooth results. As societies grew more progressive, they traded for the gentler methods of beeswax and caramelized sugaring, or razors made of bronze or flint. Even our modern versions of hair removal, those I naively thought were introduced recently, date back to the mid-1900s.

In the forties, the US spotlight shone on electric razors. The fifties brought wax strips and the first versions of laser hair removal. With the unveiling of swimsuits in the seventies came flashes of bikini lines, and in the eighties, salons awarded selfcare to their loyal clients.

So, how do women today continue the momentum of this of rich history? The women in my group of friends gather for Wax Night. We honor our friendships, pass along wisdom, and share purposefully scheduled time for rejuvenation. And..., we wax. This is a limited-invitation-only occasion, and though others drop in from time to time, we have a regular roster of six: Lynn, Beth, Ashley, Jax, Kenzie, and me.

Part One

ONE

Ready For A Girls' Night

O n a typical frozen Friday evening, I'd wrestle my boys to bed, drape into my recliner, pick up a book, and settle in by the fire. But not tonight! The posse is due to get together. Tonight, we get wild and (un)wooly.

I make my way through a nightly domestic practice with excited anticipation of the evening's shenanigans. Our little family has gathered around the table for my famous meatloaf—the kind that doesn't taste like your mother's—and now shifts to bedtime routines. Nick is out, tinkering in the shop. Both kids have taken showers to wash their little boy bums from a day in sweaty snow pants and itchy stocking caps, and from the grease they acquired handing wrenches to their dad as they helped work on the '95 Mustang 5.0 they call White Lightning.

While the boys shimmy into their pj's, I move toward the dishes and tread past the picture on the dresser. Behind the glass is an image of my mom. She has one hand under each of my infant arms while supporting my rubber neck with her fingers, our noses touching. I brush some dust from the mahogany frame with the hem of my cotton shirt, letting a thumb sweep across her cheek. Miss you, Mom.

I pass into the kitchen and sidle up to the sink to rinse the extra ketchup off the dinner plates. The muffled scrape of the neighbor's snow shovel indicates his clearing the way for another six inches of snow forecasted to arrive by morning. It's cold enough outside that the windows have a flourish of frost along the edges of the panes, intricate designs of a multitude of snowflakes. The last of the day's sun splinters through the pattern on its journey to the knotty pine cupboards behind me.

The swoosh of the back door sliding open and closed signals Nick's return from the shop. The long strides of his six-foot-four frame are echoed in the clap of his leather-soled boots. He rounds the corner and enters the kitchen sporting a faded denim work shirt and boot-cut Wrangler jeans—his everyday attire. My blue-eyed 'long-legged cowboy' gives me a playful grab on his way past. He stops and turns, looking at me with a glimmer, before bending down to give me a scratchy, stubble-faced kiss.

"You know it's not sexy to swat my ass when I'm doing the dishes, right?" I flirt, with a sideways glance.

"Wanna bet?" Nick raises an eyebrow in response. He sits at the table and places the palm of his hand on the spur ridge of his leather boot. With the skill of forty-plus years of practice, he slides each of them off and stands them by the chair. Our black Australian cattle dog, Callie, who followed Nick in, now sits in front of him, vying for attention.

"Arrrrrre you ready forrrrr a rrruffin'?" he asks, reaching down to give her a good scratching around the collar. Callie is our first-born, his treasured companion. Nick has come in the house because the parenting baton will shortly be passed his way.

Moving from the last chores of my night, my seven-year-old Sammy reads *Charlie the Ranch Dog* aloud and I tuck him in. His drawn-out yawns and giggles from butterfly kisses lead us out of the day's adventures. I turn off the lights and pop into JD's room to encourage my ten-year-old not to read too late. He barely glances up from his book to give a long-suffering sigh of acknowledgement, dark eyelashes framing the eyes of his father.

I'm now ready to strip off my domestic role and shift to co-conspirator to the girls. This night has been on the calendar for five weeks. It's time to ride.

⁂

Throwing on my Carhartt coat, and with a parting kiss for the hubby, I tell him not to wait up, and head out. The crescent moon is already stretching to illuminate each of the crystalline flakes, nearly weightless in their fluttering fall. I'm careful not to slip on the sheet of obsidian ice edged by the four feet of snow that has accumulated so far this winter.

The broom that lives beside the front door is designated to remove the snow off Nick's frigid light-denim-colored Ford pickup, often my steed of choice. Inevitably, I have to stop after three or four swipes to blow warm air into my bare hands. Wish I hadn't forgotten my gloves on the dash. I slide onto the seat of the truck and wait while the defroster melts the ice from the windshield, holding my stiff, frozen gloves in front of the heater vent before pulling them on.

Engaging the clutch and easing the truck into gear, I set out for the ten meandering minutes into the next small town to pick up Beth. She's my fiery, musically bewitching, ever-the-life-of-the-party red-headed friend. Beth and I met at school when we were eleven. She moved here from Texas. We soon realized we lived near one another and became fast friends. She's been my rock since, even moved back home during our college years to help guide me back from the brink of complete breakdown.

I pull into her driveway and punch down the parking brake with my boot. A shoulder bump and the pickup door opens with the creak of cold joints to the smell of wood smoke hanging in the frozen air. The squeaky crunch of snow beneath my boots signals temperatures below zero. There's no need to knock as I reach Beth's door; we haven't knocked on each other's doors in more than twenty-five years. It would be offensive at this point.

As I waltz in, Beth and her boyfriend, Rod, are settled on the couch in front of the TV. I refer to him as 'Hotrod.' He doesn't seem to mind the title. Although Hotrod chooses to join his better half on the couch, I can tell he's disenchanted with the show, drumsticks in hand, battering out a rhythm on the canvas foot stool. He's the drummer in their band, and Beth is the lead singer. I sit beside them, lay my head against the plaid throw pillow, feigning we will be here long enough to get comfortable, and stretch my legs up over Beth's lap with my angora socks doing a little dance over her leggings—the red flowers, green leaves, and yellow accents spreading a collage across her thighs. How can she wear floral leggings! Dreadful.

"Watching your favorite show, I see," I toss in Rod's direction after seeing *The Housewives* is on. He glares over his shoulder in a mock standoff, holding my gaze, not missing a beat.

I can't help but stir the pot a little. "Such remarkable examples of the real-life women we all strive to be." A wry grin is returned by this man of few words. "So attractive with all that plastic and plaster. And the cat fights? Riveting."

Pushing red curls behind her ear, Beth gives me a wide smile. Her eyes dance with the pleasure she finds in Rod's tolerant support of even the mind-numbingly-painful things she enjoys. He's much more tolerant of them than I: both *The Housewives* and the leggings. Beth loves them both, equally. Rod is a mellow, laid-back personality; he's her person, the one she's connected with on a level never reached with anyone else.

With a snicker and a squeeze of his shoulder, I bounce off the couch, grab Beth's hand, and nudge her toward the door. She's not one to be easily whisked away. We bundle up to brave the still-plummeting elements. Beth pulls on fawn-colored Ugg boots, negating the need for socks. She wraps a scarf around her neck and grabs fur-lined gloves. I, too, have cozy and soft leather gloves (now that they've thawed), but I'll never wear a scarf. Even the thought of wrapping my neck makes my stomach clench. I stay warm enough without one.

We jump into my still-running truck and crank the music even before I drop into reverse. It doesn't matter which song is playing. We love music, period. We belt out "Walk This Way" by Aerosmith and Beth's voice carries a tune whereas mine sounds more like the retching one might hear at a karaoke bar. I can keep time though, so don't count me out. We relish the moment all the same and our enthusiasm elevates steadily with the beat.

Just outside Beth's subdivision is a gas station. The truck clamors to the left and claims a parking spot as close to the door as possible. We pull back our seatbelts but make no move to exit, turning to each other we burst out the final lyrics and finish the refrain in laughter.

When the song hits its closing notes, we make a dash into the store for girls' night necessities: drinks, smokes for Beth, and lemon juice for Lynn's vodka chaser. The steam from our laughter freezes in front of us. We stamp our boots and head directly for the beer coolers, weaving our way through the aisles and back to the checkout line, where we run into a good friend, Evan. He asks what we're up to. Beth dishes out the minimalist version of our plans.

"Can I join you?" he asks. He bumps into a chip display and gloms onto a small bag of Fritos in hopes of making his blunder look purposeful. We girls shake our heads.

"Will there be a pillow fight?" Evan is hopelessly enticed by the picture he surely carries in his head of such an evening. He glances down and fiddles with his chips in an attempt to mask the excitement in his eyes. It is evident on his face, nonetheless.

"Do you have boobs?" I flatly reply.

"Yes, in fact, I do," he returns with a wide grin and an Oscar-worthy thrust outward of his barrel chest. "So, you're saying there's a chance?"

The lilt at the end of his sentence assures me this will be a hard-fought debate. "Nope. Let me rephrase. Do you have boobs capable of sustaining the life of an infant?"

"No, no I don't," he pouts. "But I feel like this is some sort of sexism."

The left side of Beth's smile curves as she offers the clincher. She sweeps curls over her shoulder and states, "The only way men are allowed to come to Wax Night is if they agree to wax the same things we do." With a wave, we pay for our goodies and turn on our heels to leave.

TWO

The Experience

*B*eth and I converge on Lynn's house and let ourselves in with a lyrical "Hellooo." We lift away the many layers that protect us from the cold and toss them on a bench painted a brilliant teal along the wall, placed just below a large red-orange poppy painting. Poppies are Lynn's favorite and a reflection of how she commands a room with her infectious laugh and beaming smile. Coming around the corner, donning a new pixie cut to her platinum hair and a tank top that breathes summer into the otherwise frosty conditions, Lynn opens her arms wide. Our burdens are lifted away as we embrace with overdue hugs.

Jackson has just arrived behind us and bustles in—our made-for-adventure, tough, reliable, and a bit of a bad-ass friend. Jax (we call her) works to heft her enormous purse onto the counter. A personality as robust and mighty as hers requires a body of ample size. Have you ever known a woman who's lost weight and then doesn't seem to contain the same vitality? If Jax was any smaller, her body wouldn't balance out the vivacious nature within. Her thick, luscious hair cascades over her shoulders and dazzles with its gold highlights as she makes her way to settling in.

Ashley, who came straight from a building site, sits cross-legged in the chair and sips from a mason jar filled with what we Montanans call a Whisky Ditch: whisky, water, and ice. I can't stand how stylish she looks even in overalls and a red plaid flannel shirt. Who else could make that ensemble look sexy? With her crafted exterior and small stature, it's hard to believe Ashley works her own construction company.

Exotic beauty Kenzie beat us all here. Wearing a pajama-bottom-and-knit-top combo, with her ebony hair and captivating features, she rises from her post at the table between the living room and kitchen and immediately requests the corkscrew that's been deemed an emergency tool: it travels anywhere Jax does.

Jax is obliging, in her salty way. "Hold your damn horses. Let me put my stuff down." She places her phone on the counter with a huff, next to her beverages, wallet, and a meat and cheese tray. She rummages around for a moment and pulls out the corkscrew, then is able to throw her arms open to greet us all.

"Why do you have to be so needy, Kenzie? Can't even wait until Jax's in the door," Beth teases.

"I know. But Momma needs wine."

★ ★

All of us in the posse are mothers; though not a prerequisite for the group, it certainly is a highlight on our resumes. Good thing too, because I've never needed more support and advice than I have as a mother. Being responsible for a little bambino's existence is daunting, to say the least. In our case, it takes a posse to raise a child. And wine. Lots of wine.

Our signature girls' night started so long ago, it took some digging in my memory banks to remember what got this party started. Glancing around the room from one lively face to another, I think of all the moments we've shared. We stood in attendance for one another when we wed. Then as mothers, we've shared the elation of delivering our tiny miracles into this world and have chaperoned each other's bundles as well. At least one of us has joined the celebration for each of these pivotal life events. No child of ours has been born without the arms of Momma's friend there to swaddle and croon. No wedding commenced without posse approval of the groom beforehand.

Wax Nights began when Lynn wanted to expand her services at the salon but wasn't confident in her abilities. She wanted to practice so she set about enlisting willing participants. Now, about half of us take advantage of said expertise in the comfort of Lynn's home with the company of our favorite women, overflowing drinks, and lots of laughter. Little did we know what a heavy weight this laughter would carry us through.

I've known our Lynn since grade school. Back then she had long golden hair, simply styled with bangs, and didn't occupy a room the way she does now. Tonight, her hair color is almost white it's so blonde, with a splash of pink. Lynn's a hairdresser with a long list of loyal clients. With this success she now owns her home, which, as a twice-divorced mother of three (16, 14, and 6), she has worked tirelessly to achieve.

As we make ourselves comfortable, our host skips around and curls her arms about me for another hug. I relax into the warm embrace. Lynn takes a quiet deep breath and her exhale sounds the release of tension. I step back and run my fingers through her short and sporty hair, mussing it. Her hair looks right, even when it's messy.

It's time to settle in for a night of friendship and bikini waxing. This is not what some might think. No, we don't have pillow fights in lacey bras and panties with feathers floating down upon our tousled hair. No, we don't sit around naked and rest our boobs on the kitchen table. Yes, we take off our pants, but put them right back on after the waxing's done, therefore negating the thought that our actions are akin to a nudist colony's. It's a pre-scheduled engagement about every five weeks, because who wants to wait longer than that to wax... or to hang out with their best friends?

Quiet Kenzie is presently snuggled in with her knees pulled up to her chest, her olive skin and long, lush black hair adding a sultry err to the corner in which she resides. She's drinking from a go cup—now that she's been able to open the wine bottle. We have no need for fancy wine glasses here. They clash with the lack of sophistication of the goings-on in the kitchen. Besides, we like to stay consistent in our presentation of a slightly unsavory bunch. She lingers with the dry, sweet, robust bitterness on her palate after inhaling its bouquet by placing her sculpted Greek nose over the glass. With three crazy kiddos (15, 12, and 10), and the free spirit that flows through her house, she craves relaxation more than the rest of us—a tired momma but a tireless friend.

The girls are all settled in at the table except Jax and me. She's now orga-nized enough to free her feet from her house slippers (her one foray from flip-flops) and grab a seat. She fills her glass from the same bottle Kenzie placed at the center of the table, a grocery store—yet not entirely cheap—red. I wrestle off my cowboy boots and saddle up to the table with my cup of lemon water.

Tonight, I feel better served to just drink H_2O. I've heard it said that during the coldest parts of winter, Montana has less humidity than the Sahara Desert. I haven't confirmed this to be true, but a girl needs a lot of hydration and ChapStick around here. Feeling the ache of a hangover even before I hit the sheets just makes me feel old. Also, a few of us have personally witnessed the menacing effects of alcoholism on families. For these reasons, my drinking expeditions only flash six or seven times a year, if that.

Sliding a small strand of my caramel, cornsilk hair in a figure eight around my thumb/forefinger/middle finger, I recall Beth's 16th birthday. A big group of her friends all gathered camping gear and headed up the Bridger Mountain range to spend the night. Her mom, Sarah, and stepdad set up their evening's residence in a rented Forest Service cabin and we teenagers pitched our accommodations in the small clearing below. After dark, we elevated our horseplay to include the bottles we snuck in our sleeping bags. The thrashing of tent walls and rollicking laughter alerted Sarah, and it wasn't long before she called us up the hill to the campfire, watching me haul her staggering daughter the many paces from the tent.

As the flames lit our bodies and we scuffed our way around the fire ring, Sarah glanced over one face after another, each lowered to the dirt and gravel, before zeroing in on each of us for a verbal lashing.

"Do y'all think I don't know what's going on down there? Think you're covering up the fact you've been drinking? You know better. I can't believe y'all," she growled with arms crossed over her chest, turning to face directly opposite me, the embers as my only buffer from her glower. "And, Katie. What you've had to deal with—after your mom's trouble with drinking? You certainly know better." She just let that hang in the air like the smoke from the fire, clinging to my clothes. She broke the spell of her stare, looked at each of the other campers, and continued.

"Clean yourselves up and bring all your alcohol up here. Then you're going straight to your tents to sleep off your bad decisions." Sarah had a heavyweight title belt in throwing punches of self-accountability for one's shadowed choices. She was like a second mom to me and took the job seriously, setting me straight whenever I was sliding—a misgiving then in my eyes, but a gift when remembering it now.

Our pixie, Lynn, breaks the spell of my meandering mind with the sound of the faucet. She's puttering in the kitchen preparing her vodka–water–lemon drink in a mason jar and gathering waxing products. She prepares the room, i.e., a blue foam mat on the recently swept kitchen floor with two poppy-orange couch pillows and all sorts of accoutrements. The wax is warmed and ready for action and the tools of the trade strategically placed for use. Purposefully poised on a towel within reach is a pair of tweezers, cotton balls, different sizes of strips, application sticks, and a small blue bottle of soothing solution.

"I'm glad you're all here," Lynn chirps.

We raise our glasses with a whoop.

"Beth, take off your pants. You're first."

"OK. Hold on." Beth wiggles out of the floral-print leggings I'm certain she only chooses to wear as an annoyance to me. I think all leggings are a travesty to the modern wardrobe, but floral print? Geeze!

Beth has no need to take off her socks because she never wears socks. I, on the other hand, leave my socks on while the rest of my lower half is completely exposed. I'm pretty sure we lose heat through the bottom of our feet as is rumored to happen from the top of our heads. That's my story.

Because Beth's band gigs keep her schedule booked tight, she wasn't with us last time and the length of the locks on her nether region is a testament of a full gigging calendar. There's a reason we plan each engagement approximately five weeks apart. If we wait longer, clippers are needed to trim first, which happens to be Beth's least favorite part. In fact, her face shows pure terror when Lynn reaches for the clippers on the counter.

Beth lowers herself to the mat. "Alright, Caro-Lynn. Don't you dare nick me with those things. Oh man... I'm sweating like a fat kid at the Texas state fair." She squirms and prepares the way a child knowingly contracts when receiving a shot. "For the record, yes, the chubby kid with the funnel cake was also me."

"You're so dramatic. Relax," says Lynn with an eyeroll.

I giggle when Lynn turns on the clippers and the buzz makes Beth's face screw up with worry. Beth turns her emerald eyes toward me and her gaze burns into mine with a bold glare. I find more entertainment in my friend's discomfort than I likely should.

When it's Beth's turn, she is animated in her response. Well, she's animated in her responses to everything. Beth is the biggest performer and self-proclaimed wuss of any of us and acts as though Lynn is using her as a voodoo doll, taking out a day's worth of aggression on every hair follicle Beth holds dear. But she asked for it. Beth's hardly a delicate flower when you witness this charade in person, mostly because she takes on the mouth of a salty soldier just returning from deployment.

"Son of a... Mother...," Beth sings her misery at a high C. "Seriously, what are you doing down there?!" She makes a fist and bows up as if the pain is unbearable. "Are you trying to torture me?"

This elicits an eye roll from Lynn and quite a lot of snickering from the rest of us. The other girls laugh; I giggle. My father refers to it as the sound of a chipmunk. Apparently, my giggle is one of those that's distinct yet not annoying. I'm only confident in this assertion because I have coworkers who have thanked me for coming back from vacation because they missed my laugh. I take that as a sign it's more endearing than obnoxious. It is, however, true that you can find me in a store full of people without much searching if I'm even remotely amused.

The other four of us focus in around the kitchen table and continue our stories as Lynn paints on wax and strips portions this way and that.

"OK, Jax, tell us about the latest with the Italian Stallion. Have you conquered yet at *Words with Friends*?" Beth asks to keep her own mind preoccupied while the next strip of wax is going on. We're eager to hear. Ashley makes a dramatic turn of her body and drapes her legs off the side of the chair. She tugs on the straps of her overalls, sits up nice and straight, then leans over and places her chin on her hand like *The Thinker*. She lasers attention toward Jax's bountiful figure across the table.

Kenzie, with a twinkle in her eyes and a smirk to her smile, plucks a pickled green bean from the jar Ashley brought from the garden and satisfies her salty-sour craving. She must already have some inside details to this story. The Italian Stallion is the nickname we've given the man Jax has been chatting up while playing the online version of Scrabble. She's insanely intelligent and has the most expansive vocabulary of anyone I know, executing it to perfection. It irks Jax to no end that she can't beat this guy at her kind of game. We take it as a sign the Italian Stallion's a smart cookie and we like that about him. Jax does, too, though she's hard-pressed to admit it. If nothing else, the game has started a conversation between the two of them and we're all living vicariously through their flirtatious banter.

Tossing thick brown hair with golden hues up into a messy bun, Jax replies. "Nope. I have yet to triumph. Oh, but I assure you, I will," she says with the raise of a crafted eyebrow and cascading tap of her fingers on the table. "He flippantly throws down byzantine words beyond his comprehension. I'm sure of it. Probably wields a dictionary instead of an actual intellect. Who does that? Beats me at my own game? Asshole." Jax grins as she says it. Right. If this were true, I don't think she would have sent that smoldering picture of herself to distract the man.

Ashley and Lynn have asked for that picture so they can frame it. We're all in love with how the camera angle highlights Jax's poise. The closeness of the shot, the encroachment on her personal space, bestows an air of confidence and independence. No one should be able to take such a glorious selfie. We loathe her for that mastery.

We press Jax for more details about their latest conversations. We're all fascinated with her ability to capture the Stallion's attention with words, phrasing, intention, and her photo.

As the night progresses, conversation rises and falls like instruments tuned to one another, each getting solo time. Sometimes we allow ourselves the relief of a good cry over painful situations that have risen since the last time we were together. Some of us cry for the situations in which we find ourselves, some of us merely in empathy. Most of the time, however, is spent in robust and side-splitting laughter.

We have an unspoken tradition that around midnight, Lynn crafts tortillas with cheese, pitches them under the broiler, rolls their crispy shells, and places them on the table with sour cream and the favored brand of hot sauce. Our playlist fades to background music as we gather around the table. The calories sustain us in sharing all our lives have to offer.

When all energy is spent and my cheeks are tired from the workout of laughter, it's time to head home. Beth and I forge through the heart of the Rocky Mountains that surround the valley, driving the frontage road to her house. This is a prime time for deer to be out nibbling bark off branches within their reach as they continuously move to keep warm during the frozen months. We keep careful watch of the fields and ditches for any who might dart into the road.

I drop Beth off and drift down the road lit by the crescent moon, with the rhythm of the night's conversation replaying in my mind. I'm rejuvenated and ready to step back into my role as wife and mother with a full heart and a silky-smooth undercarriage. I enter the door to my home and I'm serenaded by a crackling fire in the hearth. There's something about the heat of a wood fire that offers a general feeling of solace. The warmth weaves its way through each room, infusing comfort into every corner.

Light from the flames dances on the couch, inviting and entrancing. The amber colors glint off the six framed pictures that adorn the adjacent wall. Each exhibits an action shot of my husband aboard a bareback horse, hand raised high in balance with the horse's movements, tan and teal chaps flying as he tries to clinch that round of rodeo. As flickers reflect off the glass, it's as if each image is animated and brought to life. I curl up in my chair, caught in a reflective pause, and wonder about this life we've created.

When I at last tiptoe to my room, I hear muffled snores. Before allowing my favorite silk jammies to fall over my smooth and sexy skin, I massage my legs with lotion. The soft lavender aroma encourages a deep and relaxing breath. I crawl into bed and slide down between the sheets. Nick turns and reaches to put his hand on my thigh, pulling me closer, still sound asleep.

Many nights, such as this, I go to bed and wonder what earthly thing I could've done to deserve all this. Might it be that such joy can be earned through the pain I've navigated in my past? Does the universe match depths of sorrow in balancing measure? Perhaps tragedy, with time and healing, has allowed me sight to witness the treasures in my life, and to warm myself by the embers of gratitude. Whatever the reason, tonight I sleep with the comfort of friendship blanketing my soul, soothing me the way Mom's down comforter did when I was young.

THREE

Building and Tending the Fires of Friendship

*T*he posse has gathered around the hearth of a community we built, taking turns tending and stoking the fire. During weeks, months, even years where we, as individuals felt the bitter cold of loss or despair, others kept watch over the coals to provide ever-present warmth, and defense from errant sparks. We've tended our relationships faithfully after crafting them with much care. We built these friendships via different avenues: shared childhood history, tough trials and triumphs, and the commonalities of women.

⚹ ⚹

Beth crooned into the phone the lyrics of "Crazy".

"Uuugghh," I responded. I'd stayed up too late and we had a test in eighth grade English that day. "How can someone wake up crabby when you're singing Patsy Cline?"

"Alright then, get your ass out of bed and don't make me late. Oh, and come in because Mom has a blueberry muffin for you to eat on the way," Beth urged.

I arrived as on time as I ever was, and we bumbled off to school, hefting our backpacks into place on our shoulders along the way.

"Why can't she just give us a ride?" Beth complained of her mother.

"Because we have parents who are mean and think it's fine to make us walk. And apparently below-zero weather, blizzard conditions, a hundred miles don't matter."

Beth and I met in fifth grade. What are now her copper curls, at that age, reflected the stick straight nature of youthful indifference. When she moved here, she brought a vibrant Texas personality with her. We became fast friends and discovered we lived in the same neighborhood so I could swing by her house on my way to school and we'd walk together. Beth called my house and woke me with the same song each day. We stopped by the gas station on our way to school for gum and candy, and Taco Bell on the way home. Beth ordered hard-shell-meat-and-cheese-only tacos every time.

Beth and I have a long history together, but Lynn was the first companion Beth gained when she moved to Montana. It took a few months for Beth and I to bump into each other on one of our passes through the shared neighborhood, and it wasn't long before Beth, Lynn, and I started spending time as a trio. Our usual tenor was that of Lynn glancing above the pages of her book to oversee Beth's lyrical performances along with my cheerleading.

With each following year, we three explored the mountains on Lynn's family ranch and soaked in the hot tub staring at the stars through the steam pluming up into the sky. When our bodies flushed from the heat of the water, we'd jump out in a cascade of laughter and roll in the depth of the snow before hurling ourselves back in and squealing with tingles.

When we were in high school, Beth and I watched while Lynn participated in taekwondo competitions and cheered her on from the sidelines, wishing we had what it took to pursue something that required such confidence and strength. Confidence and strength have been Lynn's friends far longer than we have.

At Beth's house, we danced and sang. Sarah, Beth's mom, had a collection of vinyl records she treasured. One of our favorite pastimes was to crank up the music. Our first album of choice was Fleetwood Mac. We watched Lynn dance to her favorite, "The Chain." She would sway and clap, and then at the climax of the song, throw her hands in the air and spin with such exuberance, the whole room expanded.

My house was most often a pitstop on our way to adventure. Mom always had food to nourish us as we passed through—fresh bagels, cookies, bread, and granola to name a few—all homemade and doled out only after paying the toll of hugs and conversations about the goings-on in our lives. Her outlook on parenting was less structure and accountability, and more belief in the responsible nature we possessed. Such a belief didn't always work to our favor.

Mom was laid-back and had a jovial personality, lubricated by her natural disposition and the drinks she inevitably had under her belt by the time we arrived at our house. The girls welcomed the reprieve from lectures about grades and curfew. They leaned into Mom's heart and generous assumptions of our natural ability to make sound decisions. Many nights we spent whispering of boy crushes, daydreaming, and giggling over racy excerpts from Lynn's latest romance novel, our cheeks flushed. Beth was often the center of entertainment even in our small home.

* *

Friendships can go through a lot when we're young women, especially when growing into ourselves, or avoiding growing up at all. Between hormones and loves and so many shifts, switches, and moves, remaining true to ourselves, let alone our friends, proves daunting. Friendships are not always positive or easy. Often bringing too many blooming women into the same circle means playing with fire, which also brings the risk of getting burned.

* *

The friendship pairing among us that has lasted the longest, and spent the most time together over the years, is Beth and Lynn. Their personalities after high school, however, grew in different directions. Lynn, with her solid foundation of confidence and strength, headed in the direction of maturity right off the bat—hers was a heart that strove for kindness. Beth, on the other hand, learned to cover her pain with hard-edged sarcasm and dramatics as the tethering of her family began to unravel. Her parents divorced when she was young, and just after high school her mom had recently divorced a second husband. Beth didn't have a strong relationship with her father, strained by a lack of ability to communicate. She ran from the deep-seated pains and fears relating to those things as fast and as furiously as possible.

The duo was spending time together after high school when Lynn started to notice glaring incongruities in their personalities. They would be walking through the shopping mall and be on two opposite planes when it came to interactions with others. Lynn strived to be positive and uplifting. "Wow, I love that girl's outfit. I wish I had the confidence to wear that style."

"Are you kidding me? Just because they make those pants in her size, doesn't mean she should wear them," Beth said with a toss of her hair.

"Be kind," Lynn countered. "There's no reason to be mean."

"Yeah, well... truth hurts, I guess."

Lynn tried for many months to champion her steadfast friend out of this critical frame of mind. Beth's emotional wreckage would not allow for such a mature perspective to sink in. She was blind to the impact of her words and actions, lost in her meandering travels. Lynn felt the person she loved, and the essence of what cemented their friendship, was no longer within reach. For her, the apathy Beth showed was too much to tolerate. This left her brokenhearted and determined to push through with healthy confrontation. Lynn wrote her a letter:

> ...At this point, I feel the only thing left for me to do is ask that we take time apart from each other. I don't want the person you've become in my life. I want the person I fell in love with ten years ago, but I feel that person will take some time to come back around.

Those two didn't talk for three years. Beth wasn't invited to Lynn's wedding. Lynn had no idea when Beth moved to Arizona, and then back again. After going through what was on par with a painful separation, a lot of growth on Beth's part, and a chance meetup while downtown, they spoke again. On that night, they stepped out the doors of the brewery together and the pattern of their shoes made momentary prints on the wet concrete of the patio. The rain fell as they shared a cigarette, each taking long pulls before passing it back to the other. Drops from above spotted the shoulders of their coats and dampened their hair; drips ran down the sides of their faces. They finished talking, embraced, and stepped out in stride once more. They left the past behind and have been close ever since.

⋆ ⋆

We three moved our separate ways after high school, through our own tearing down and rebuilding processes. Lynn went to cosmetology school and spent her time building her career and a marriage she would later leave. Beth moved to Arizona, shacked up with an abusive partner, and funneled herself further down the drain of self-defeating action. I drifted aimlessly through a year of valueless relationships before enrolling in college and incrementally enveloping myself in the company of cowboys that shared livestock management courses. After years during which the smudge smoke of immaturity clung to our shoulders, we reunited and again turned to our friendships. Now the kinship constructed during our early formative years and the nostalgic moments bring us closer.

Ashley and I met while I was in college. Her companionship offered a visage of self-assurance, courage, and drive, the likes of which I'd never before witnessed. She knew how to have fun, how to love without reservation, and how to do all things on her own terms. When all the other college girls were fawning over young men and clamoring for attention with outward displays of grandeur, Ashley adorned her small stature in Carhartt and plaid, just as she does now. Led by her inner drive alone, she traversed a path she herself pioneered. With each decisive step she trekked confidently into her future.

With frolicking-filly days behind us, Ashley and I grew our friendship while growing our families. During the trials and triumphs of several rites of passage—marriage, pregnancy, and first-time mothering—we were drawn together. We walked beside one another from good-time girls to wives to mothers, becoming sisters in experience, sharing moments that are customarily only offered to those within the constraints of bloodlines.

We've remained close while she and her husband, Wyatt, built up their construction company and now partner side by side building craftsman styled homes. Ashley works physically harder than any woman I know. It came as no surprise to me when I learned that the people at the landfill call her "The Unicorn." That's right, at the dump. Ashley drives the construction trailer to unload its cargo in the middle of a mudhole and does it better than the rest of the big, strong guys that come to do the same. When she pulls the trailer into the dump, jumps out looking like a Carhartt model, climbs like a monkey to the top of the lifted trailer, and dangles down to kick the frozen cargo loose... let's just say she's a sight to behold. She's been asked twice to please come down before she gets hurt. Those darling boys know nothing. I've been a witness to these magnificent attributes for two decades now.

Tenacity is a common theme for the posse. As career women, Lynn and doe-eyed Kenzie worked side by side at the salon when they were just starting out and have worked off and on together since. The shared hours at the salon offered them time to build on what they knew of each other's lives and learn the value of their personalities. Beth and Jax made spirited next-door neighbors and opened the doors to each other as companions, often through invitations to birthday parties or summer BBQs. They both share the gift of incredible singing voices and the love of music, and the invitation became a standing one. The marvelous four: Lynn, Beth, Jax, and Kenzie started to develop close-knit friendships as a group, as well as individual pairings.

Sometime later, when Lynn was first separated from her second husband, she and Kenzie arrived at the depths of kinship forged only by way of searing heartache. Kenzie stopped at Lynn's house every evening after work to check in and crawled onto the bed to run her fingers through Lynn's honey-platinum hair until she'd cried herself to sleep. Kenzie brought nothing but her heart, framed by her dark features. She held Lynn's hand until she could stand the day, the week, the month on her own. Through shared vulnerability and tenderness, they forged bonds of friendship that have held strong ever since.

During shared festivities and girls' nights out, we all six came to spend time together. It's this kindling of connection that ignites the limitless potential of friendship. Although Lynn and Kenzie no longer work in the same salon, Beth and Jax have moved to opposite sides of town, and Ashley and I have our most momentous life events behind us, we're still able to keep strong bonds forged in the daily rhythms of the ordinary. We do this through regular hours spent together, and in the traditions of our ancestors—waxing and wine. It's a hard-won celebration.

FOUR

The Spark of Differences

*T*hank you, social media, for justifying cliques of like-minded people and making us ever more sure that we, alone, are right. Through the guise of unity, it seems as though the general thread carried throughout our social conversation is one of either piling up cliques of group-think or drawing lines in the sand. Seems there are a lot of people who search for like-minded companionship, same backgrounds, religious views, lifestyles, hair styles, fashion, interior design... undies for God's sake! It's easier to get along with people who share similarities. Yawn.

Isn't the point to life not about who's wrong or right, but rather about finding a place of belonging and vital comradery? During a time in our nation when a vast number of people are bent on proving we're unable to work through differences or disagreements, it feels monumental for our posse to prove otherwise.

I cannot tell you how valuable it is to have friends who disagree with me. Flint and steel must first collide before a spark is rendered. The friends who've become like family to me have many differences. We didn't choose to spend time with one another because we share similarities. Instead, we chose to come together with, and in spite of, our differences and allow them to bring us closer. In our case, these differences make us whole.

The posse hails from various backgrounds. We vary from generally Christian to the specifics of Baptist and Catholic, to women who are spiritual but not religious. We have staunch Republicans in our group. Jax is an NRA-membership-holding, take-no-government-handouts-while-she-is-breathing, gun-toting (in her MacGyver purse) type of woman. We also have left-wing-minded women in our group—the types that use essential oils and believe in a woman's choice. Some of us raise our children in a democracy, some of us a dictatorship.

We are women of moderate income, and median income. I personally grew up receiving boxes from the local food pantry to make family meals for Thanksgiving and Christmas, packed with canned pumpkin pie filling and cranberries, a turkey, and a sack of potatoes. Our educational backgrounds vary from college degrees, trade degrees, to high school degrees. A few of us spent our teenage and college years on the straight and narrow, or with noses buried in books. Others had misspent youths during which we made decisions that may have been frowned upon. With all of these disparities between us, it's hard to imagine us getting along famously.

We do, though! The fact that we have such varying experiences and backgrounds adds many layers to our friendships, a collective encyclopedia of experiences as a resource. With the adventures we've each encountered, this is a resource of remarkable depth. We were all brought up in small-town Montana. This being the case, it's worth saying that we still see life from radically differing angles. Given such, we're often asked how we do it. How do we hang out and share life as women and as families for the long haul, without division?

I was taught by example from a young age that the best way to learn is to listen to opposing sides of a topic. My dad's an environmental activist. His work is that of saving forested areas from logging, grizzly bear habitat from encroachment, and many other valuable endeavors. But he's also lived the opposite side of these matters. He was a logger himself at one point in his life. The fact that he has, through his own eyes, seen both sides of these issues is of the utmost value in being able to objectively evaluate such heated topics. Through this lens, he taught me we don't have to agree on controversial subjects, but if we don't listen to the other side, we must ask ourselves how we can be truly educated on our opinion.

Sharing opinions and engaging in debate can be rewarding if done within the constraints of fairness. The trust we have for one another is one of the reasons Wax Night is held closely to a specific short list of names. Within this roll call we have proven character that allows for debate and shared vulnerability. The personalities of the women on the roster are more important than the number and the names.

Another element paramount to the success within our group is a keen awareness that severing the humanity from which the argument grows, from the argument itself, can incinerate a debate down to the ashes of cruelty. The back and forth of debate that can bring life to a friendship can easily turn to its demise if one does not consider the heart of the person sharing their opinion. The freedom of expression these strategies allow is invaluable. Imagine a place where you can kick off your flops, pour a cold one (all the way to the brim), let down your hair, drop your pants, and say whatever comes to your mind. Well, nearly whatever.

* *

Lynn is an example of how one's rearing and current course can meld beautifully into a balanced perspective. Although her casual, college-relaxed style of dress doesn't depict the upbringing of a cowgirl, she comes from a conservative ranching background. She grew up raising cows and her parents' right-wing beliefs, based on generations of this lifestyle, showed daily in the labor of her dad's hands and the fatigued chocolate leather of the checkbook cover, worn by hours of placement between her mother's fingers. It's ingrained in the tapestry of who she is.

She still believes a great deal of these truths. For example, she decided to take a women's firearm training course, which allowed her to learn more about firearms and apply for a concealed carry permit. Her decision to take the class was dually driven: she wanted to have a permit in light of today's political climate and wanted a way to further her personal growth.

I come from a much more liberal background, and not only from my dad's point of view. My mother exhibited her liberal mindset through an investment of time and energy as well. She worked tirelessly to accelerate the growth of the community food co-op and contributed a contagious enthusiasm and engagement in the community gardens. Mom and Dad both shared their free spirits and in-depth dialog with nature through their intimacy with Native American virtue. I learned a great deal from the fervent ways they championed these beliefs.

Like Lynn, I eagerly searched for my own education with which to supplement the foundational beliefs built by my rearing. Early on, I came to find the ranching lifestyle to be one that speaks true to my heart, as if a bestowal far before even my birth. I've followed the conservative path it leans toward, balanced with the love instilled in me of nature and its rhythms. I don't find these points of concern to be mutually exclusive. The spiritual, life-giving energy I find in the connection of my soul to a chestnut saddle horse joins in harmonious song with the heartbeat of the wild lands upon which we ride.

Lynn and I both consent to the fact that the ranching lifestyle is a hard one; it's an extraordinary way of life and gives back in a way that cannot be duplicated. We don't, however, have to agree on all related issues. I don't have to concur with the hunting of wolves as a response to their predatory nature, for example. She doesn't have to find merit in their placement on the endangered species list. We both feel the greatest spiritual introspection on the top of a mountain—she via a hike and me atop the freeing energy of a horse. And yet, we don't experience nature's sanctuary the same. She holds in her heart the closeness to the Lord, Jesus Christ. I nourish my soul with the universal and loving energy of nature.

Oh girl, we're very aware these are heated topics with a lot of impact on society as a whole. We acknowledge the things we say may be disagreeable to some. We don't intentionally say hurtful things; we have to play nice. No drama for the sake of drama. No stirring hard feelings. No "girl" stuff.

We're not judgmental of each other's perspectives, agree or not. There are precious lessons we can teach one another. I see tremendous value in the fact that my friends are committed to their beliefs and the things they feel to be true. They find the same value in my commitment. In doing so, we can get along without cat fights, gossip, or division. Whenever those things do rear their ugly heads, we call them to the table right away. Not only do I appreciate this, I count on it. It's important to know for certain if I do inadvertently hurt my friend's feelings, she will allow me to fix it.

Why, in a general sense, do we treat differing opinions with a trembling hand? The Montana women I know don't sidestep problems. We work hard, get dirty, and do what needs to be done. We don't apologize for the way we lead our lives, steadfast in our commitment to our livestock, animals, and communities. We don't gently move cows with lulling music and tender touch. We rope and herd and run them through the chutes, love them, and care for them, but don't need a dainty touch to do it. We are grown-ass women.

Between transitions to professional jobs, getting married, and having children, women go through a tremendous number of ups and downs as we get older. Maintaining friendship equilibrium amongst all of this can be a juggling act, one which can result in dropping a ball or two. I'm certainly a chief offender in this regard. Though our posse does have a kind of ethereal relationship for the most part—and I do not exaggerate my depictions of support, love, and comfort—I must say, we are by no means perfect. Our R-rated comradery has not come without its share of turmoil.

FIVE

By No Means Perfect

I've been told numerous times that we cannot love others better than we love ourselves. Truth be told, I have long struggled to achieve such inner compassion. To be honest with myself has been a struggle, hindered by my inability to rely on the legitimacy of my own reality. At times, I've been completely incapable of reading the words written on the chambers of my own heart.

An unrelenting sense of despondence grew with intensity as my second son grew within me. Was this depression? It runs in my family and I'd been keenly aware of the possibility that it could affect me too. As I'd soon learn, during pregnancy I'd developed postpartum depression (right? It's not limited to after Baby is born). Because my emotional instability was caused by a chemical imbalance—a hormone-induced depression—there was no 'thing' I could do to fix it. And I didn't figure any of this out right away; it took me longer to realize what was going on than I'd like to admit.

In the meantime, I came home from work on my lunch hour day after day and sobbed uncontrollably—no cause, no tangible reason for my sadness, nothing needing repair. This was the only margin of time I didn't have to hold myself together for my family or at work where I had to be professional, the only time I could allow myself to let out my unending feelings of sadness. Unfortunately, this meant they all came out in a torrent.

I tasted the salt of my tears the moment I pulled away from the curb at work, settling into the corners of my mouth as I drove home. Entering my house, straight to my room, I threw myself on the bed and clutched my dusty-green comforter as a child clings to the soft cotton of a blankie when being pulled from her momma's arms. And I'd fall apart, lying there with my knees held to my chest by my arm's embrace, until I could no longer put off going back to work. Dragging myself toward the door, I'd glance in the mirror as I passed by the bathroom, praying I hadn't blown blood vessels in my face.

Each day I was determined to figure out what was causing me so much sadness and how on earth I might fix it. I searched and dug and clawed to find what was eating at me. I asked my husband for support, but he didn't have a way to fix something even I couldn't identify. I cried out to Lynn and to Beth. Anyone, please, just tell me! I spent months appealing to my friends to hold me up, taking from them any energy they had to spare and giving nothing back.

Ashley was my closest friend at the time, and I went to her with my frustrations, fears, with my inability to recover. At first, she gave me a ton of advice and tried her best to help in any way she was able. After weeks and weeks of my sadness, she had to do what was right for her by spending less time around me and not calling often. She needed to create some separation between us so she was not continuously frustrated with me. She simply could not understand the darkness, though she tried.

From my shadowed corner of the planet, it appeared as though, during the time I needed her the most, my closest friend turned and silently moved away. Many nights I sat up and thought about how angry this made me, how hurt I was that she would distance herself when I was growing a child within, clinging to any chance of hope or clarity. Uncertainty of my value in our friendship coupled with the gloom I was already feeling. My tears eroded further the chasm growing between us.

I was driving back to work one day, after another of my exhausting meltdowns over my lunch break, and I thought about Ashley and our friendship. I drove past house after house, street after street that led away from my current position. I recalled one effort after another Ashley put forth to sustain me and decided to pick up my phone and call her, selecting the 'favorite' from my list of contacts.

I started the conversation by stating I needed her honesty. I hadn't heard from her in weeks. I asked straight up if she was avoiding me because I was so sad lately, because the balance of give-and-take seemed to be weighted on my end of taking. I could tell it took all her strength to answer me truthfully.

She simply said, "Yes. I'm sorry," then paused and allowed a widening silence to enter the conversation. After what seemed an exhaustive amount of time, she went on. "You've been negative and not yourself. I don't know what to do for you and can't handle seeing you so glum. So, yes, I have been avoiding you. Whatever this is, I can't help you with it. Maybe you should call your doctor. I'm remembering your mom, and Katie, you need to take care of yourself. You can't keep thinking you will get through this without help."

What I needed in that moment was not a soft shoulder or a placating answer. What I needed most was to hear the truth. If Ashley hadn't been willing to tell me the painful truth, I would likely have gone on months more wondering if it was me that was broken or everything else. Nope. Confirmed. It was me. I called the doctor the next day.

"This is Katie Dawn and I need to talk to Dr. Anderson about the possibility of help with depression."

"OK, let me connect you with her nurse."

"Hi, Katie. Tell me about what's going on."

"I don't know. I just feel like I can't get over this unending sadness. I don't think it's circumstantial." I described how I was just plain sad, how I thought it might be depression and that I needed to get help. "I'm worried about meds and the fact that I'm pregnant, but at this point I need to make sure I'm healthy, too."

"I understand. Do you feel like you are a harm to yourself or to others at this point?"

"No. I don't."

"What is today? Monday. Can you come in Thursday at 9:00 a.m.? Just a moment, hold on...."

I could hear Dr. Anderson in the background. Her muffled voice a comfort in and of itself. "Wait, Katie? We'll see her today, especially given her family history. Make time in our schedule this afternoon."

"Can you come in at 4:00?"

That day I was prescribed a low dose of an antidepressant after a long conversation about the difference between emotional/situational sadness and the imbalance leading to chemical depression. Ashley's honesty was the irrefutable evidence I needed to reach out for help. I needed the truth, and she was the only one strong enough to offer it just then. Even while unable to dry my daily tears or walk beside me through my darkness, what she was able to offer was more valuable.

On a lighter note, and more related to everyday imperfections, Ashley's also the kind of friend who will call and say that before you drive an unfamiliar tractor, you should make sure you know how to stop it. Mostly, because she learned it the hard way, and fixing fence is a bitch—especially when it's someone else's fence. And, as specifically stated in her call, she wanted to make sure I knew she does stupid shit too. God love her. She isn't perfect either.

* *

We've all encountered times when we were not our best selves, and the truth is, we can never be healthier than the sum of us. Our posse has chosen throughout the years to extend to one another grace and forgiveness. As importantly, we've helped each other forgive ourselves. Not one of us, after all, is perfect.

SIX

Smoke before Fire, before Warmth

There are nights when we wish only to be found, to be little girls once more, so we might lie down again in innocence. But sometimes life takes us places we'd rather not go, or we dance with danger and wander too far, until we feel entirely lost. Secrets such as these shape us into the women we've become. Frightened and alone. Baring such secrets can set us free from their stronghold.

⋆ ⋆

Though I had solid friendships and spent time with good people, during my teens, a dangerous incongruity burrowed its way in and claimed a home. The questions that thundered through my mind during that time were reflections of not just teenage angst, like many kids my age, but also of a cavernous kind of broken. *How can I spend time with people and yet feel as though the connections I make only seem to strengthen the depth of my longing and ache?* I wondered. The more I worked to build value in relationships, the less value I saw in myself.

I grew up in Bozeman with my mom one school year at a time. This was considered 'city' life for me, though the global estimation of this sentiment is laughable, really. This town, nestled in a valley surrounded by expansive and high-reaching mountain ranges, is where my two brothers lived with Mom and me; one brother, Matt, is three years older, and the other, Luke, is three years younger. We all shared a mother, none of us a father in common. It was just the four of us, our fathers having left Mom to raise us alone, and mine the only one that shared in the task of parenting. Every other year, I would nest with Dad in the foothills of Kalispell, a valley about five hours from Bozeman, leaving Mom and my brothers behind.

During the months I lived with Mom, I rambled around downtown with my girlfriends, got lost in movies at the theater, and raced around the roller-skating rink. We girls spent hours at town parks and festivities and congregated at the bungalow-style drugstore, with its ice-cream counter and red and silver spinny stools, for root beer floats.

We strolled through the infamous Cactus Records store on the weekends. It offered all the music we could possibly crave. Moving to the back of the store, after flipping through our favorite artist's records, we dashed from one intriguing toy to another, placed our hands on the static electricity globe, wondered at the lava lamps, and coveted the fake vomit pranks. None of us had any money, but the exploration of what could be kept us enamored for hours.

While in Bozeman, I attended school with classes of thirty students, two and three classes to a grade, striving to be included at the popular lunch table. This was offset by the ever-fading two-room schoolhouse experience in Kalispell, where I was the one child in my grade, lumped into an outpouring of close-knit community. It was a K-8 school occupied by some twenty kids in total. We marched across the playground to the gym/cafeteria, washed our hands, and gathered home-cooked meals prepared by one of our teachers in a kitchen that resembled our own.

My dad's property was out of town, along a then-dirt road. While with him, I was given the gift of spending time in the foothills of a different set of mountain ranges where I fabricated dams in the creek, peddled miles of dirt road, galloped on horseback along the fence lines bordering the vivid cadmium color of canola fields, constructed forts and teepees from tree limbs in my forested backyard, and trekked to mountain tops. Country living at its finest.

When I was just a tyke, living with my dad allowed the backdrop for this naked little girl to occupy hours picking honeysuckle flowers on tiptoes and sucking the sweet juices from their stems. Dad could find me by tracking the trail of marred flowers across the property. Several creeks provided a world of wonder where I rounded up snakes, turtles, and frogs. Neighboring lakes gave me the space to grow swimming and kayaking muscles; rivers were my classroom to hone rafting skills. The comfort and calmness of Dad's property tendered the yearly delight of spotted fawns nestled down by their moms in our backyard, as well as cover for bears and mountain lions to explore on their ambling way through the mountains. The soul of Dad's place is still a safe haven.

From an outside perspective, and a practical one, this family arrangement was ideal. I was able to spend quality time with both my parents and develop routines in both homes, differing largely from each other, offering a wide range of perspective and learning. I experienced the excitement and buzz of town living in tandem with the freedom and restoration of the country. With a plethora of experiences from which to draw inspiration and creativity, I was extended the favor of getting to know both sides of my family and connecting with them for a whole year. In many ways this balance was a tremendous gift.

My parents offered every opportunity they could muster and tendered treasured time with both of them. The logistics, the equal time, and the bounty of love shown from both sides were definite feats. There has been scarcely a day in my life I haven't believed my parents did all they could for me. Seldom do I doubt the undying fortitude of their devotion.

However, what I've come to realize as an adult is that the jockeying back and forth between homes created in my young self a soul who—when looking into the mirror of her being—saw only a sunken reflection. What seemed like a romantic upbringing left hollow spaces that I tried to overlay with reflections I found in others' gazes upon me. The continuity a child craves with regard to connections with family and friends had gone missing. As I look back for answers to explain the angst and emptiness I often felt, I uncover a much different image than the ones displayed in the scrapbooks of my youth.

Now as I transition into the maturity of age, and I examine the entire composition from which I was crafted, I see the canvas of my heart as a whole picture. To not appreciate each purposeful brush stroke and varying shade of the portrait—the darkness, brilliance, and intimate detail—is to dismiss the artistry of the creation. The practical gifts of my situation show in warm amber colors of various shades, while emotions splinter in hues of indigo and cobalt. Finally discerning the dark shades of my portrait allows me to experience the full depth of this masterpiece that is me.

For the first time, I am allowing myself to feel my past, not just remember the events: the road trips Dad and I took, the baking Mom and I shared, classes, schools, teachers, Grandma's house down the lane. The heartache too. When I moved back and forth between homes, I had to get reacquainted with every person in my life all over again, every year, only to forsake them the next with a great wrenching sadness. A chasm of loneliness. I would then reveal my new self to my family on each side of the divide and try to reestablish our relationships. In doing so, I experienced the ambivalence that accompanies detachment—something required for my heart to weather the yearly severance.

The sustained effect of these darker hues on my growing personality brought an insatiable craving to find true depth of connection. In sixth grade I made the decision to stay with my mom every school year, finally securing a stage to cultivate long-standing friendships. I hadn't developed the tools with which to do this, however. I didn't know how to purposefully choose friends, to determine what a true friend acted like. And I didn't have the self-esteem needed to buffer those who would capitalize on the desperate desire for familiarity I gained from not only my back-and-forth commuting, but also by being the child of a parent with addiction.

During my teen years, I threw myself at anyone who tossed a glimmer of attention in my direction. A select few were driven by their inner compasses to treat me as a true friend, Beth and Lynn among them. Mostly though, I surrounded myself with people drawn in by my desire to be all they needed or wanted. As the daughter of an alcoholic mother, I added a dash of an enabling and codependent spirit, and I was off to the races in giving more than I had, to people who gave little back.

Through my navigation of high school, my so-called friends and the boys I surrounded myself with took advantage of my vulnerable willingness. I became lost in the quagmire of unhealthy relationships and choices. Without my parents' knowledge, when I was just thirteen, I began to hang out with a group who were five and six years my senior. They were 'friends' in that we occupied time together and therefore didn't feel alone. Otherwise, there wasn't much this bunch of screwed-up drugged-out delinquents had to offer. I was inexperienced and trusting, and they welcomed me with open arms into their world. Fresh meat.

One of the guys in this crew was Jake. Jake was attractive—tall and charismatic, with a hint of dark and hollow ghosts reflected in his eyes. He presented himself as older and wiser. Many in the group looked up to him, so did I. He was eighteen to my thirteen. Given my naivete, my physical and mental inability to make healthy life decisions, I was flattered when he offered me his bed one night, so eager was I to feel the comforts of innocent affection, drawn in by my changing hormones. I called my mom and told her I was staying at a friend's and she didn't doubt me.

Jake's version of these comforts was much different than mine. Jake had one more emphatic yes than I had high-pitched noes. I lost my virginity that night to a man who lost no time getting his needs met, then rose from the bed, went to the bathroom, and dusted off his nose while shuffling back. Jake lost no sleep when he lay back down beside me.

By the time the sun rose the next day, I had decided on the version of the night's events that would make me look the most grown-up and the least violated. I bragged up my loss as if I'd earned a badge. I covered up the excavation of my innocence with the storytelling of a child. Though never an excuse for such an occurrence, this was the direct result of choosing friends who were broken and as badly in need of care as I, and pouring myself into them. I gave all I had and left the rest on the floor.

Because I was looking for intimacy with not just a boyfriend but also friends in general, I opened myself up to hurt from all directions. Later in high school, there was a girl I came to spend a great deal of time with named Casey. She was a little cowgirl too and her family had some land just outside of town, a few horses, and leased pasture for cows to graze. She was rough and tumble, just like me, though rougher around the edges. Seeing our commonalities, we started spending hours together in the evenings and on weekends. The friendship started out as mutually beneficial. We both offered companionship and she was willing to share time on horseback, something that brought light to even the darkest places in my soul.

Our time spent with the horses allowed my spirit a deep cleansing breath. The horse's lather soothed my aches and pains, the rhythm of his cadence acted to calm me like that of a grandmother's lap and rocking chair when I was an infant. Long weekends we spent handling the horses, gliding our hands across and around all parts of their bodies, building kinship. The worries of my life were held at bay by the fences within which we rode. We practiced barrel racing and pole bending in her arena. Casey taught me much about handling horses and sitting a saddle. I absorbed every molecule of healing from those miraculous creatures. I was in heaven; and pieces of my heart were being restored.

One evening, we saddled the horses for practice on barrels. After much invigorating work, we decided to ride down the road to the brand-new gas station on Ferguson Avenue to get ourselves a Pepsi. She held my reigns while I strode into the store. With our goodies gathered, I stood in line to pay, and a man behind me noticed the spurs on my boots.

"Fueling up the Mustang?" he said.

Amusing.

"Gonna let her buck" was my only reply.

After some time, Casey began to take out her temper and aggression on me. She, too, came from an alcoholic family and one that felt neglectful. She accumulated power in our relationship as I relinquished it. She'd known me long enough to trust my devotion and feel my desperation for company. I was an easy target, though I'm certain her aims were not consciously divisive.

On one occasion, she asked me to do something for her, or possibly with her, that I wasn't inclined to do. What it was I don't specifically recall, but I know it wasn't a huge ask. Her reaction when I said no, however, was the ending of our close friendship, and the trust necessary for it to survive. Casey knew how much spending time with the horses meant to me, knew the weight of the gift she offered in sharing such an opportunity. I'd been verbose in my statements of gratitude. When I said no to the request, her answer ripped a hole in my chest: "You either do this or you won't be welcome to ride out here anymore. You don't want that, do you?"

It was as if she snatched away the one thing that had given my heart some peace amidst a tumultuous childhood and held it in front of me with a sneer, held this life-giving gift as ransom for my servitude. She bucked, I bailed. With the strength of little more than an ounce of self-preservation, I walked away. Even broken souls have lines that cannot be crossed.

SEVEN

Take Off Your Pants

We can choose to sift and sort and make meaning from past relationships. As for me, I tweezed out what I can keep and what I won't repeat. After a checkered past of intimacies, tried and failed, I choose to be surrounded by these five women. Given the nature of the friendships we've built in our posse, though, I can be surrounded by these five women—one of them working closely with parts of my body I've hardly studied myself—and relax into a feeling of safety. I enjoy Wax Night for the comfort and friendship, but I do enjoy the results of waxing as well. I get bad stubble rash when I shave, and it used to be a constant aggravation. When I wax, I'm graced with a silky-smooth feel without irritation. And, yes, I opt for more than just my actual bikini line.

I mostly do this for me. The time and attention feel like an invigorating secret—the healthy kind—a way of pampering myself that is evident for weeks (although, I guess there are choices that don't include stinging moments of torture). And, my husband appreciates the art of the tidy landing strip I request, as a side benefit.

Even though I can get waxed around my girlfriends, I still won't consider getting waxed by a stranger. I've never even tried. I'm not one to wax a stranger either. All five of my senses agree—it's not a job for me. I'll stick with the mundane paperwork of my day job.

Before I get too carried away in describing the confidence building our group has achieved, let me say there's a practical aspect to all this. How can we make too much of our weight or body image while spread eagle on the kitchen floor, holding one quivering thigh up in the air with the other propped on the oven door handle? Even if no one peeks, taking oneself seriously is hard to do in this position. When waxing, there's little interest from anyone in how the extra weight on my arms jiggles when I wave or how my pants create a bit of a roll over the waistband. Hell, I'm not even wearing pants.

When I was first invited to Wax Night, I was apprehensive. I'm a reserved person by nature—a definite understatement. If I'm in a room full of people I don't know, without a job to do in the constraints of the gathering, I shake with shy nervousness. I fumble at small talk and feel awkward and exposed, and that's when I am fully clothed.

Before gathering in this manner with my friends, I hadn't tested the mettle of my faith in close friendships to dissuade this unfavorable feeling of exposure. I hadn't ever truly revealed myself to them, and by this, I mean the caverns of my heart. I longed to have a more authentic depth of trust that allowed me to do just that. I was at a juncture where I wanted to strip off my layered defenses. By then I was happily married, had a successful career, and was residing on a stable foundation for what seemed the first time. I had an opportunity to take advantage of this unwavering landing point, to flex the muscles of my wings, and to dare to fly.

✶ ✶

There was a time when I was younger that Mom nudged me out onto the outlying branches of the nest, assuring me of their stability, while standing close by to offer a sense of safety. Though I recoiled from social recognition, Bozeman, an artsy, bustling university town, offered plenty outlets to develop a well-rounded expression, one being the Miss Teen Montana pageant. I still find it hard to believe that I was willing to be in the spotlight, yet the tangible evidence in my childhood scrapbooks gives proof.

At only five feet, three inches tall, I never considered myself the type of person built for a pageant. Although I do have long legs for a short girl, I don't have particularly intriguing features or a refined presence. But out of the hundred girls there, I made it to the top sixteen. Twenty years ago, I looked the part more than I do now.

After I received the letter stating I'd been nominated to compete, Mom helped guide me through the process with pride and steadfast reminders of my value and all-around beauty. She had little money to spare, so we traipsed around town together and collected sponsors to support the endeavor. One of our larger clothing stores (the only one in town with an escalator) lent a mature and vibrant red satin dress for me to wear. It hugged my hips and with a subtle slit up the leg was elegant in simplicity. The shoulder straps were an inch wide and their supple texture accentuated the draping neckline.

I have a picture of me in that long, flowing dress framed on my wall. In it, my mom and dad stand in admiration beside me. This picture is one of four I have of all three of us together. It captures one of a sparse number of times we gathered for no other reason than to celebrate one of my accomplishments. It felt foreign. It felt exceptional. I'm always surprised at how outwardly I looked the pageant part when the inside portrait was of a quiet and burdened soul. Little did I know at the time, but this outward presentation was a version of me I would one day grow into.

I was a rough-and-tumble tomboy type in my everyday routine. I wore Wrangler jeans and cowboy boots and was often either covered in dirt, mechanic's grease, or hay. It was all I could do to dust off enough to be somewhat presentable at work. When I lived in the dorms, I carried the saddle my dad gave me after graduation up and down the elevator of my dorm room as the textbook I needed to fulfill my horsemanship class. It nestled at the foot of my bed each night, covered in a multicolored saddle blanket. My roommate and I set up our roping dummy on the front lawn of the dorm to practice our skills in the afternoons. I would never be caught in pink, or lace, or dazzles.... So, I kept this extracurricular example of my demure and ladylike self to myself.

One Wax Night I let the secret slip. I mentioned how the satin dress I wore for the pageant reminded me of the time Mom and I spent together creating the costumes for a different endeavor. Belly dancing.

"Wait," Kenzie demanded.

"You did what?" Jax asked.

"Yep, this little cowgirl was a belly dancer. I can show you a few moves, if you'd like," I said with an exaggerated circle of my hips.

"Well, I never...." Jax stared at me as if investigating my features for the first time. "Quite the disparity from the Katie of my previous acquaintance. What other treasures are you hiding?"

"After all these years together, Love, I'm glad I can still surprise you. But I warn you, all of you. Tell anyone and ruin this gravelly reputation of mine, and you'll regret it."

I described how I danced at the biggest festivals in Bozeman, how Mom and I sewed our own costumes, including the mesmerizing gold coin bras that were the tapestry of choice for the profession. "She had many more coins on her voluptuous bra than I did; wealthily endowed if you will. Mine sported mere pennies' worth then."

I twirled the small section of my hair that had fallen out of my messy ponytail between my thumb and ring finger, making a figure eight back and forth as my mind reached for the memory of working together, crafting our attire. I pictured Mom reaching over the table to place her hands over mine and guiding them through the twists and turns on the sewing machine. I leaned into this motion like an embrace. Her golden corn silk hair framed her face, enhancing the gold flecks in her amber-hazel eyes. My finished garments were dainty, long, and thin. Hers were curvy, robust, and sensual. Though built with contrasting proportions, we both felt resplendent in our garb. The swell of her pride for me on performance days, when we shook what the good Lord gave us, was unmistakable. We reveled in the sheer delight of being with one another.

Though the belly dancing and pageanting sides of me were not ones I readily disclosed, during those times my mom reflected a vision of me, a part of me that was true, and that which remains. With the glimmer in her eyes as she looked upon me, she proclaimed I was worthy of celebrating and offered a mirror by which I could catch glimpses of my beauty.

✶ ✶

Throughout the following years, I entered an interval when my mother's face was no longer a looking glass for viewing my significance, and my self-image grew more shadowed, scratched, and pitted. I allowed the mercury of Mom's reflection to become tainted by others' oxidized impressions and with my own self-imposed degradation. The haunting memories of that time are still vivid.

* *

Ninety-eight pounds and falling—the point at which I was smallest in stature and in spirit. I had a long rutted, washboard road ahead, fighting with myself, my physical presence and my weight.

EIGHT

A Heavy Burden to Bare

*W*hy can't you find even an ounce of self-control? You don't need ice cream. Look at yourself. If you don't want to be disgusted anymore, either don't look in the mirror or maybe just don't eat the damn ice cream. You choose, but these are your options. You have no willpower. Right now, you're failing miserably.

I've been plagued with inner commentary such as this, punching myself in the heavily insulated gut over and over, for decades now.

You think you should go to the twenty-year high school reunion seventy-five pounds heavier than the last time most of your classmates saw you? That's almost two times as big as you were.

I know, I know. I was anorexic then and unhealthy.

But seriously, two times your previous self? Imagine what they'll think.

Maybe they won't notice?

How could they not? Just stay home. You'll be more comfortable here and they won't even realize your big ass is missing.

We know comparing oneself to others is not a good idea. The thing is, comparing myself to a previous me—all's fair there, isn't it?

Whatever. You got married, comfortable, complacent, lazy, and now value yourself far less. Maybe just get your ass off the couch and do something about it. Get your shit sorted, lady. It can't be that hard.

Alright! I've had enough.

The real question is: How on earth did I let myself become deeply committed to such an abusive relationship with myself? Have I always been this mean?

No. When I was twelve, I remember feeling thin and pretty. But that can't be right. That's when I took my first steps toward falling into anorexia. None of this makes sense. If I truly felt thin and pretty, why would I even consider eating a problem, or calories to be my enemy, and therefore start starving myself? I'm confused. Who's driving this bus, anyway?

⁎ ⁎

When I tried to put my journey with anorexia on paper, I was primed with outward societal words and connotations. I wrote an entire chapter on weight and my troubled relationship with it. At first, I reasoned that I ate less so I would be thinner. Eventually I recognized my flawed thinking, grew healthier with the understanding and slowly allowed myself to eat again and regain my strength, though the disease still has an emotional stronghold on me.

My statements in those pages were succinct; eating less made me thinner, decreasing the self-consciousness I held regarding my appearance. That was where it all started. Isn't that the globally understood accelerant for anorexia; a general dislike toward outward appearances, driven by societal expectations and definitions of women's beauty and value?

I read my original chapter many times over, expecting the expression of such darkness to heal as it had in other arenas. But my words seemed empty of true recognition and offered no such healing. My story rang hollow and lacked authenticity. These observations needled their way deep into my thoughts, puncturing the integrity of my writing. The pinholes drained the trust away, and truth went missing in the retelling. The pure essence of my deep-seated emotions was nowhere to be found. I had to go back, start over. Writing, scribbling, erasing, going back. Crafting the telling with unencumbered words allowed veracity to come forth.

The latter part of the story, pitted with self-deprecation and insecurities regarding my physical appearance, is an honest depiction of my struggle. I do still grapple with how I look in the mirror and don't see an accurate reflection of my size when I stand naked. Obese, unattractive, enormous. These are some of the feelings that come over my heart if I study my stature for too long. My arms are wide and underneath they wave when I do. My stomach is anything but flat and my waistline is no longer flattered by jeans. It's a good thing I have a very tall husband (other than the fact that he's a full thirteen inches taller than me and weighs less) because when I look up at him, he doesn't see my double chin. Instead, Nick is drawn in by the one part of my body that gained confidence with weight: my breasts.

Logically, even I know that 'obese' and 'enormous' don't accurately describe me. I own a scale for one reason; I need evidence. Am I really that overweight? The scale assures me I'm not. Would I look upon another woman's five-foot-three frame, at a hundred and seventy pounds, with disgust? No. Something's definitely skewed, amuck, crossways in my brain and such damage was done by a disease called anorexia, a companion of mine for far too long. Because my body shrank down to a mere ninety-eight pounds when I was young, any greater number now feels repugnant.

If that's honest and true, what am I missing? After much searching, I hunted down the scurvy lie. My anorexia didn't start because I thought I was fat. 'Fat' is a word that landed in my vocabulary as a result of anorexia, not the other way around. Tricky snake. No, for me, anorexia started from a much different narrative than the culturally built derivative.

The spirit of the young teenage girl that was me, was in turmoil. It was confused, broken, and emotionally emaciated. I yearned for someone to truly see me, to help me. I cried out for sustenance. With immaturity and the media as a guide, my emotional constitution devised a plan. If people couldn't perceive the withering of my soul, maybe they would notice the withering of my body?

The descent into anorexia began with my inner self clamoring for an outward, tangible manifestation of its pain. I've known people who've waged similar wars against themselves in order to garner recognition of their inner angst. I knew a girl in high school who used razors to etch her inner pain onto her outer being. When she allowed someone close, they bore witness to the turmoil within. A feeling of physical pain is concrete—the depth, the reason, the ways to make it stop. As is the feeling of hunger.

⋆ ⋆

Here was the tragic flaw in my plan. When a young woman gets skinnier, it's most often seen as sexy; encouraged, praised, championed. I was desperate for emotional nourishment, so I starved my body in hopes someone would notice and offer the sustenance I needed to feed my soul. The plan worked. I was noticed, unfortunately. Noticed for my slimmer build, flatter stomach, for the way I fit a size-two pair of pants. The surface was noticed with even more intensity than before. The depths were shadowed further. The value of the attention I gained for my smaller size far outweighed the depravation. And so, it ensued. My eyes darkened as I was fed by the empty calories of physical attention. I had no energy to defend my honor, and I was left with even less of myself with which to cry out.

⋆ ⋆

As I grew into adulthood, I dusted myself off and got back in the saddle. I turned the reigns toward the horizon of healthy relationships that I knew existed because, in hindsight, I recognized a tiny shoot of belovedness planted in me by my parents and other role models. Many dusty and weary miles I traveled to where I now rest. I had many things to learn, landmarks to register on the map of my heart, sunrises and sunsets to spend getting to know myself. I rode by windows that reflected a maturing face, one whose cheeks began to round with health and eyes that shone with a new vibrance. I collected pieces of value for myself that I could then tender for shelter. Eventually I had a place to hang my hat and a rough-sawn table around which I could build community. It was here the posse gathered. They ducked in the doorway, pulled up a chair, and stayed for long conversations over strong coffee served in tin cups. We then knelt before the fireplace, or sprawled along the hearth, and found comfort.

As a now-forty-year-old mother of two, and wife, I have been able to slowly gain back my physical health. My return to feeding my body resulted from extensive time in therapy, tending the emotional wounds that drove me toward anorexia in the first place. I learned I had a vision of physical self that was unhealthy, learned my perspective was skewed. But no one person or group of people can reverse such a disease. Mere companionship isn't strong enough to rewire a brain with such damage.

For me, now knowing that my thought process defaults to 'twisted and rotten' changes the way I look at unravelling things. With this perspective, I have become focused not on changing my weight but on changing how I think about my weight. This may seem like a small difference in phrasing, but it has made an enormous impact on my struggle. I now work daily at changing my negative self-talk instead of changing my outward appearance. When I start to think negatively about the way I look, instead I offer myself a gentle grace. *It's ok. Be kind. You are magnificent. You don't need to change. Please don't be mean to my friend. It breaks her heart.*

✶ ✶

In my mom's absence, the women of my posse stepped in and offered me her mirror of recognition. I was reminded of the beauty I held within. I saw what beauty looked like on me, through their eyes, tried it on, and it fit to size. Now, I am comfortable enough to bare all in front of them.

Just as these women see amazing things in me, I behold them, dazzled by the way they carry themselves. I am encouraged by the true visions of beauty they encompass. I believe they, too, garner courage and strength in my reflection of who they are.

Lynn, for example, is our sunshine. Her pixie haircut sparks excitement in her sage eyes that flicker with laughter. Full, round cheeks accentuate her beaming face. Both exude her kindness at a glance. She has the most radiating smile of any of us and shows a caring and quiet acceptance with her move-ments and posture. Lynn is the personification of grace, readily offering it to herself and encouraging all those she encounters. She brightens a room the moment her body makes an entrance.

Jackson is our diamond, sometimes in the rough. The glimmer of her azure eyes is driven deeper with a gaze that draws you in as if whispering to you a secret. She can rock both ends of the spectrum, from coal to precious jewel. On occasion Jax wears a bad-ass messy bun and a comfortable tank top with the catchy phrase "Good at Bad Decisions," all the while wielding sarcasm like a saber. Other days she polishes to a shine, dazzling, brandishing rays of intelligence and sophistication. She draws people into her presence and keeps them there, enamored by the dichotomy of which she is made.

Kenzie is our exotic beauty with dark, intriguing features: delicate olive skin, a narrow face, long chestnut locks, and forest green eyes. The group's sometimes-unexpected surprise, Kenzie is more reserved and introverted than the rest of us. A master of fluidity, she ebbs and flows with life, moving between situations the way water moves through mesh. Her energy quietly ripples throughout a room as a smooth and sultry tide. When she does create waves, we surf, only returning after a great adventure.

Beth, a rockstar, is ever in the spotlight with a voice that can be explained as a bestowal from God. Her spirit reverberates with every word she croons. Her vibrant copper hair frames emerald eyes, and porcelain white skin is dusted with the occasional freckle for depth. Her youthful energy is shown in the bounce and underlying rhythm of her gait, reflecting the vitality and playfulness she brings to any endeavor. Her personality exudes the 'everything's bigger (from) Texas' slogan, and her jovial nature can bring the house down.

Ashley, our unicorn, a mythical creature. No one can quite explain how all that beauty is contained in one soul. She's all things alluring: strong, healthy, and energetic, the perfect balance of femininity and strength and looks just as remarkable in woolen overalls as she does in the little retro dress claimed at Goodwill. Her hair is gilded with highlights atop chocolate undertones, from many hours working and playing in the sun. She cannot walk into a room without being noticed because the depth of her character and kindness stride right in beside her as an outward manifestation.

My friends are beautiful women of different shapes and sizes. Their mental and emotional health radiate outwardly in the most exquisite ways, showing me that confidence looks much better on a woman than size-two pants. There's seldom a time when I'm around these women I do not feel gorgeous.

We've discovered the secret of feeling at ease with our pants off in front of each other. And... how I've come to feel mostly content in my own skin.

Instead of seeing what I see in the mirror, I see the reflection of their love for me, all of me, in their eyes, bright and clean and clear. I've leapt from the perch of my foundation and found flight. The gale force winds that pummeled my past are behind me. I now have the strength and courage to play in the gentle breezes that follow such raging storms and allow them to lift me. These women stood by me throughout my tempests. Now we play together and rejoice in the updrafts of friendships forged through courage.

Alright, ladies. After all this hard work, who wants to dance?

NINE

To Dance or Not to Dance—
Is Never a Question

"*E*veryone can meet at my house and I'll drive," I declare in a group message to the posse. I encourage them to get a little crazy without having to worry about making it home safely.

"I'll drive as well, but let's converge at your house," Jax quickly responds. She always drives her own rig. She's a bit like Danica Patrick in the way she flies down the pavement.

"I'm not riding with Jax. I may not make it home alive," Ashley teases. "Last time I rode with you, Jax, I saw my life flash before my eyes."

"You know I'm an exemplary driver, so shut your blasphemous mouth," Jax curtly states in her own defense.

Lynn, our law-abiding, rule-following safety agent agrees with Ashley. She will undoubtedly be riding with me. Though she has pink highlights, a rough-cut-feminine hairstyle, and a bit of an unrestrained dress code, she's unwilling to compromise when it comes to reasonable safety decisions. Kenzie just goes with the flow and is often the only passenger in Jax's vehicle.

"Alright bitches, let's get this show rolling," Beth adds in her typical foul expression of excitement.

"I'll put some pizza in the oven so we can eat before hitting the road. See y'all soon," I conclude.

One after another the girls congregate in my humble kitchen. Nick is used to the open-door policy I've cultivated and no longer remembers we have a fully functional doorbell. As each member of tonight's gathering enters, they give generous hugs to Nick too, and then snuggle the boys. We grab some plates and assemble around the room for sustenance to carry us through the night.

"Geez, Lynn. Are you making love to that pizza?" Kenzie asks with a wide grin. Lynn has a way of savoring food that makes us all want to be a part of the sensation. She takes a bite, and her gaze draws inward.

"Mm-hm. You aren't?"

Nick blushes a little. "Time for me to go out to the shop." As he exits, he shakes his head and turns back laughing with fondness warming the crystal blue of his eyes. "Be careful tonight and have fun."

⋆ ⋆

We have one hell of a good time when out dancing to our favorite band, El Wencho. Tonight, they're playing at the Sacajawea Hotel, the focal point of festivities in Three Forks since 1910, with its white clapboard exterior surrounded by a stately wraparound porch lined with wide, ribbed columns. The welcoming broad staircase in the front leads into the molasses-colored hardwood floors and white trim of an old-time hotel lobby. Our boots, however, sound on the narrow wooden steps to the side of the porch, that lead us downstairs to the bar. We fit in well with the back-entrance kind of crowd.

As we swing the door open and saunter in, our voices and laughter fill the air. We immediately relish the general feeling of hometown as the bartender greets us. "Huckleberry vodka and soda tonight, ladies?" he says with a smile that slowly builds across his face as he gathers each of us in with his gaze. "After all, I'm not supposed to give you shots this early—or so you said last time you were leaving." He gives us a sly nod and brings two glasses up to the bar.

"I'll have my usual, barkeep," Kenzie tosses out, her dark complexion somehow brightening at the thought. "Cranberry Vodka." He laughs and starts with a shovel of ice. It clinks in the glass and he moves on to the bottle. He's become quite adept at humoring us. It comes with the job description.

What makes these nights especially fun is that Kenzie drops her mom jeans and puts on party pants. Kenzie's momentum is the ingredient needed to turn an enjoyable night into an unforgettable one. With a quiet, but robust personality that can sway chandeliers, Kenzie's strong sense of presence is a force, moving our mountains of stress and responsibility back just enough to let the river of excitement swell.

These are the only times Kenzie allows herself to really cut loose. On our special nights out, her babies are cared for and she doesn't have responsibilities other than allowing some much-needed rejuvenation. She doesn't get too crazy. She just dances and laughs and has a couple drinks, drifting about the bar, becoming more talkative and feistier with each song played. On these nights, she allows us a window into the unreserved side of her personality.

This more boisterous Kenzie surprised me when I met her the first time we all went out. After many nights when she rested comfortably at the back of the table and professed to be the last person on earth willing to drop her pants in front of us because she was such a prude, this Kenzie came forward and set the night on fire. She's set to do the same tonight.

We all get drinks, start our tabs, and move to get the best possible table for interacting with the band and quick access to the dance floor. We move away from the high-top tables to the more accommodating tables closer to the stage. A cardboard statue of John Wayne looks over us from the other side of the bar, a comedic addition to a room otherwise decorated tastefully with Charlie Russel's most famous depictions of the Wild West placed six feet apart along the walls above the barnwood chair rail. We settle underneath one of my favorite paintings, titled *A Tight Dally and a Loose Latigo*.

As the night charges on, we're so invigorated by the music and company that the exercise for our hips, feet, and hearts can often be counted as hours-long aerobic workout. We end up hot and sweaty, but exhilarated and radiant.

When Beth's not playing a gig with her own band, she joins us out on the town. The boys start to sing "Single" and, under the splash of lights spilling from the stage, we all join forces. Magic happens when Beth and Jax merge their high-energy and incredible vocal range with the band, and together create a party on the dance floor. Beth's copper tendrils bounce with the beat and Jax's bad-ass personality translates through her confidence in the crowd.

"Hey, hey, maybe bein' single ain't so bad. A whole lot less of his B.S. A lot less drama baby I confess...." This song has been crafted by the El Wencho boys to engage the audience in rhythmic clapping at the end of each chorus. When we are cued in by Josh's increased vigor on the congas, we don't miss a single beat and raise our hands, putting forth all our vitality.

Though the rest of us join in singing, we don't contribute to the overall levity of the songs like Jax and Beth do. So, we put to use our other strengths. When Ashley and I were in our twenties, we burned up dance floors across the county. I happened to be the more reserved of the two of us, more cautious and responsible. I tended to lend an "I don't think so, missy. All these boys can't handle the competition," like the time she was dancing with several chiseled cowboys throughout the night after a fun evening of rodeo watching.

Funny how things haven't changed all that much. We still set our heels on fire. At this age and stage in our lives, it looks a little different. Instead of grabbing any ol' cowboy with half a talent for dancing, we draw boundaries in consideration of our husbands and only choose to twirl with the men whose feet move, and hands don't, ones that honor the rings on our fingers. A side effect of this boundary is Ashley and I often choose each other as dance partners. This has three results. One, we get much more done in a night. Two, my husband is graced with me taking the lead by autopilot when we join for a two-step in our kitchen because that's what I am most familiar with. Three, it's often assumed Ashley and I are a lesbian couple. Fair enough. We're comfortable with all three results.

Ashley and I are noticeably good dancers. Mostly because I've spent so much time on the wooden floors of enticing establishments throughout my life. I can't sit still. My body reads each beat as an invitation. The physical act allows my heart and soul to promenade as well. It's a good thing I always have dance partners within our group. Ashley, especially, makes me look good. When you lead a unicorn around with one hand on her shoulder and one against the small of her back, it doesn't take much to get noticed, what with all that sparkle and fairy dust.

Kenzie and Lynn hypnotize when they join us for their favorite songs. With every molecule in her body, Lynn vibrates with joy as radiant as the red poppies in her foyer. She swoons back and forth to the music, then throws up her hands and spins round and round, energy expanding the room and invigorating the rest of us. Kenzie's energy ripples underneath, each wave being propelled by the luscious sway of her hips.

When we finally do sit together at the table, we carry on conversation often without words. Without the necessity of backstory, we clamor on with interwoven conversations, three and four around the table at a time, all of us contributing. There are often more than just the six of us in attendance melding into one magnanimous soiree.

Tonight, Jax is garnering lots of attention. With a few of the girls already out of our seats, a cowboy hat comes sauntering over.

"You wanna dance?" he gruffly asks and holds out a hand.

"No, thank you," she replies with an obligatory smile.

"Come on. Just one."

"I'm sitting this one out, but I appreciate the offer."

The gentleman caller places his hand on the back of a chair to stabilize his swaying. He moves in closer and his eyes flash with the frustration of rejection. "What's the matter? You too good for me?"

"No," Jax replies, setting her shoulders solid. "I don't want to dance with you. Better off asking someone else."

"Fine." Spittle flies as he turns and walks toward the back of the bar like his ankles are made of Ramen.

"Man, he's drunk," I say as I lift my eyebrows to Jax.

"Nah, he's leftovers," she returns.

"Leftovers?"

"Yup, leftovers. That guy will sit in the back and no one will touch him until finally he's thrown out for being nasty or taking up space."

"Here's to never being leftovers, girls," Beth says, raising her beer bottle to the middle of the table. Our laughter resounds above the volume of the band as our glasses come together, and Josh tips his black fedora to our table.

The guys in the band refer to us as The Wolf Pack. This is not to insinuate that we're savage or predatory. Who would think such things of our dainty mannerisms and coiffed exteriors? No, they call us a wolf pack because we protect each other and work as a troop, as well as care for one another's babies. We work in synchrony, not letting anyone stray. Each of us is a part of a bigger whole and feel confidence and safety in that knowledge. Simply put; we take care of our own, and on occasion get a little wild and maybe even howl at the moon.

More than once, the limited estimation of the prowess of our pack has been exemplified. One night we were getting ready to leave after an evening of entertainment. The rest of the girls were outside awaiting their driver and I was settling my tab for a burger and four Shirley Temples—don't judge, my drink of choice is both nostalgic and delicious, and I was driving. I was leaning my elbow on the bar, foot placed on the iron step just below, when one of our friends walked by and stopped to talk.

"Have you seen Steve?" he asked.

"Yes," I responded. "He's outside with my friends. Makes me a little nervous having him out there all by himself with those girls."

"Don't worry about Steve," he reassured me. "I've known him my whole life and he's a good guy. Respectful."

"Oh, honey," I countered with a giggle. "You think I'm concerned for my friends? That's sweet...." And naive. "I'm more worried for Steve. Two of those women are single and the group as a whole is more than one man can keep up with." I patted our friend on the back and walked away as he stood there with the look of a freshman on his face. It was adorable.

As our current night comes to a close, we exchange gratitude with our local friends for sharing such a fabulous night. Josh and John, the guys that make up the band, give us hugs and we thank them for such a magnificent evening. They reaffirm the gratitude they feel toward us for elevating the momentum of the previous hours with our energy.

We head home and decide it might be the best idea ever to have a sleepover, for those of us who can. We drop Ashley off so she can sleep a little before engaging in some productive, hardworking builder thing tomorrow, and Beth so she isn't completely useless for her band gig tomorrow night. The rest of us retire to Lynn's house and settle in for a good old-fashioned slumber party.

We gather on the couch and Jax comes out wearing a messy bun, jammy pants, and a hooded sweatshirt, makeup still on point. It's nearly 1:00 a.m. and she's still going strong. She tunes up a playlist and cranks the music. The nightcap of choice is "Ice Ice Baby." With the first bass notes, Jax throws her hood over her head and partially over her face and places aviator sun glasses with one fell swoop, for greater affect. She strikes a hip-hop pose, hits a few beats with hips and hands, and then belts out every last lyric. She doesn't miss a single word and entertains us with her vocal skill and expertly executed moves. That's our Jax! Saves her best for the after party.

As we settle in our various sleeping accommodations, we intuitively know those lying in this room can be called upon any time we need them. We rely on one another. We have proven history upon which this trust was built. There was one time in my life, in particular, I needed friends more than anyone or anything else—much beyond the measure of the past struggles I've shared thus far. These women surrounded me, cried for me, buffeted my heart with their strength, and led me to safety with their wisdom as our guide.

Part Two

TEN

The Rituals of Change

*T*hroughout the world's many different cultures one can see evidence of rites of passage that mark the transition to adulthood. In Western cultures, time-honored practices have been put in place to navigate this precarious journey. Native Americans set boys to course with Vision Quests. Left alone to find a site for such an expedition, the boys of the tribe spend days building their courage and strength. They sit for hours, gazing upon the licking flames of fires they build, looking inward for answers from their ancestors as to the value they will offer the world as a whole. The ancestors speak directly to their souls, appearing in visions and the dancing of smoke, and molding them from the inside out.

Girls coming into menarche navigate their own journeys. Boys fast; girls feast. Boys are left to their inner drive; girls are surrounded by the women of their tribe to celebrate the life-giving power bestowed upon them. Moving into womanhood is an opportunity to share stories of pregnancy, birth, and mothering. Sacred are these gifts. Generational resources are handed down and cherished over the sustenance of food and familiarity. Kneading fry bread, gathering berries that stain their fingers light purple and red, and the delicate work of applying brilliantly colored beadwork to tiny baby moccasins are tangible ways these women share ancestral inspiration.

The basis for each of these rites is the same, as was the basis of the rite of passage set forth by the cowboys of the West. Boys become men on long cattle drives. Riding and working cattle side by side. These sometimes-month-long treks were opportunities to build the young individual. Boys rode for days, with too-big cowboy hats shading their faces from the sun. They naturally came into the ways of hardened men as they navigated, wrangled, wielded weapons for food and learned tender ways to connect with steed and lulling cow-calf pairings—the ways of the West. Left in the company of only the unyielding strength of nature to either sustain life or claim it, boys grew into men. They returned to their homes and strode back through the doorways changed: proud, strong, weathered, the darker hues of surmounted hardship blazing in their eyes where innocence once sparkled.

Out in the country, when the men would leave for long periods of time, girls were encouraged to cultivate the roles of women in their absence. Overalls covered in child's play were replaced by dresses covered by aprons. Spritely ramblings in the meadow were traded for sowing seeds in the garden. Great Grandma's hands shone in those of a young woman's as she and Mother crafted sustenance to fill the mouths of babes much younger. These labors of love allowed girls to transition to the work of women, tending to the land that bore all possibility, cultivating an understanding of how to flourish by their own ability.

✦ ✦

Three aspects of coming-of-age-rites remain the same throughout cultures far and near: separation, transition, and return. Separation is the step of withdrawing from one's environment, societal role, or status in order to become familiar with the new. Transition is the stage of finding a purpose by which to move forward and preparing for the change of position in the community or stage in life. Return is the reintroduction of a changed self, the crossing of a threshold to a new stage in life hopeful with anticipation for the future.

We carry within us an undeniable basic human necessity for communal rites of passage. Ceremonial acts, or celebrations of change and growth, remind us of the sacred nature of life. Generations come together to share wisdom and ritual, richly rewarding individuals with a sense of belonging and renewal. Without these stepping-stones laid before us through such rites of passage, we as a culture become wayward and confused. Left to the foibles of unknowing civilization, young souls are often brought too early into change or are left with no hearth to return to.

ELEVEN

Nothing Could Prepare Me

*If the fires that innately burn inside youths are not intentionally and
lovingly added to the hearth of community, they will burn down the
structures of culture, just to feel the warmth.*

—Michael Meade

There was no storied meaning or passage, no sense to what I am about to bring to the page. What I'm alluding to is a life chapter nearly impossible for me to summon, not only because of the pain associated with it, but cognitively so. The trauma itself has led to a certain amount of amnesia—a seemingly strong word to use—but true, nonetheless. These are years of which I recall very little. Yet I feel it's important to include here with as much honesty as I can muster because this is a story about friendship and the ugliness from which it has the power to release us.

⚹ ⚹

Being known, and the freedom it brings, comes with a price. What I'm about to reveal now feels like a series of failures at best, betrayals of myself at worst. I've stared at this line in the book for some time now. How many minutes or hours have passed? Some chapters are just too messy and sad to dive right into.

⋆ ⋆

I was nineteen when I was led down this portion of my journey, living with roommates in an apartment and going to college for an agriculture degree. Beth was off to Arizona, Lynn was settling into her career and family, and Ashley was a mere pup in high school. I wouldn't enjoy the acquaintance of Jax and Kenzie for another decade.

At this juncture I was working two jobs, had an amazing boyfriend, the kind dreams are made of, and was taking advantage of the freedom of youth to enjoy life. My little brother, Luke, was sixteen and living with our mom across town. I visited them while striking out on my own. Still, I clung to my mother's advice, love, hugs, and her goose down comforter when I wasn't feeling well.

Our almost-twenties is a time when we check in at home but don't spend a lot of time there, stretching wings, self-centered independence, and all that. For me, the reasons for not spending a lot of time at my mother's house were two-fold. First, I too was exploring life as a new adult, working hard, spending a great deal of time focused on schoolwork, and building relationships along the way. The other reason, I worried, was a selfish one made up of a young maturity and few tools built from experience with which to handle big problems and hard situations.

My mother, as I came to later understand, was struggling with the debilitating symptoms of mental illness. She had been diagnosed with bipolar disorder and paranoid schizophrenia in her early twenties. We, her family, were completely unaware of her previous diagnosis at this time. Due to the rigid privacy laws with respect to sharing this kind of information with anyone other than the patient herself, there was no way for us to know. Mom had chosen never to reveal this, and throughout life she was left to deal with the symptoms on her own. Until now, she drank to self-medicate. Until now, it seemed to work.

No one in Mom's world was privy to her struggles with mental illness. She kept it from my dad when they were together, masked it from two husbands, and didn't share with even her closest friends. She was an artist at shrouding private pain and darkness.

While other college freshmen planned to attend the Alpha Gamma Rho (the agriculture fraternity house) fall extravaganza, I was growing consumed with worry for Mom. My mother's choices, ways in which she was carrying out her daily chores, or not carrying them out at all, as well as outward manifestations made me increasingly aware that something wasn't right. I often came home to find a week's worth of dirty dishes in the sink and Mom in bed, reading a book. Other times, she hefted all the electronics out on the porch because they were damaging her brain: the microwave, TV, radio, alarm clock, and phone. Mom took Luke around, showing him vehicles she'd buy for him when "paid for the internet work" she'd done, even though her bank account had little more than a few dollars, and she knew nothing of how the internet worked. All of these things alluded to a frayed mental state.

I hate to remember, let alone tell, of these difficult truths. It was dreadful seeing my mom, through no fault of her own, become someone other than her true self. The retelling reflects a merciless sickness, one I find nauseating even while putting into words.

How does a nineteen-year-old see the presentation of her mother's mental illness in a larger perspective? How does a young woman, not yet twenty, know how to deal with the crumbling framework of the person who should be holding the entire family together? I didn't know what to do and I didn't have the strength to make a decision.

I checked out as much as I could, in good conscience. My closest friend at the time was Oakley. She helped me escape by allowing me to be a college student, to pretend I was free of such weighty matters. She didn't ask hard questions, didn't press me about what I was going to do, and encouraged me to relieve some stress on the dance floor.

When things started to get really bad, though, I had to do something. Since the resources for families of those struggling with mental illness are so few, and ways to get help are scarce due to privacy laws, after researching my options, I was left with just one.

I was not legally allowed to talk to Mom's mental health doctors in order to get help for her, and because she was not in a right state of mind to see she desperately needed help, I was left with just one option. I couldn't believe there was only one option, one decision left to make. My mother was no longer able to care for herself or my little brother. I was worried for them both.

I called the police to report my mother was a danger to herself. This meant I had to be present at our home while they arrested her, put her in a cop car, and drove to the hospital to be evaluated and committed to a mental facility. As she stood beside the back door of the cop car, escorted by a uniform with a badge and a gun, the drole of the dispatchers in the background, I witnessed the dignity and strength drain from every part of her being—face turning to that of an abused child being punished for something she didn't do. I turned away only to see Luke, just sixteen years old, holding his skinny knees to his chest as his body shook on the porch swing, unmasked fear in his eyes.

My one decision then led to the next, and the next. While my mother watched from behind the defendant podium, I was left to stand, shoulders in line with hers—our eyes never meeting—and testify in front of a judge that she was mentally unfit to care for herself or my brother any longer and should be transferred to a mental health facility. I then walked over, closing the cavernous gap between us, and handed over a bag containing the necessities for a long stay. I hugged her with such heartache and remorse that my knees buckled. Hardly able to stand, steadied only by sweaty palms pressed against the indifferent mahogany of the court desk, my chest banged so heavily with guilt, it crushed any chance of breath.

That's how it happened. I had my mother committed to a mental institution. I went through my days as if nothing had happened, as if I hadn't just made the hardest and least defensible decision of my entire life. Survival makes a strange bedfellow. How could I truly defend such a decision at that point? I knew nothing of Mom's previous mental illness diagnosis because she'd never shared such a secret. I couldn't be sure that what I recognized as a deterioration of mental capacity was the true reason for her actions and incapacity.

There's no blood test for such a disease, no confirmation. I had no tangible defense, just my juvenile sensibilities and the research I'd pored over in the college library frantic for answers. If she had diabetes—even cancer, as horrible as it is—a test would determine the level of sickness and pave the course of treatment. There are no such definitive answers for mental illnesses, nor clear-cut determinations with regard to treatment. The look on her face... arrested... a cop car... a judge... being held at a facility against her will... without any proof that I was even doing the right thing. How could this possibly be the right choice? My heart and mind were tortured by ambiguity.

Oakley was the one person who allowed me the space and understanding to check out of that frightful reality and do something that might possibly give me enough energy to take on the next day. She allowed me the friendship I vehemently needed at the time and encouraged me to take my mind off of the harsh realities of my situation. She was beside me every day, steadfast, supportive, and sympathetic, understanding of what I needed to get out of my own head.

I continued to go to school, do my homework, work two jobs, pay my bills, pay Mom's bills, help Luke, and pay rent and utilities at Mom's home so he still had a roof over his head. Our big brother, Matt, was living in Washington at the time. I worked to negotiate the legal realm of mental institutionalism with my mother's granting of a power of attorney privilege so I could be included in meetings regarding the doctors' work and opinions of her health.

I visited her at the facility when I was able to, though each time I walked away with deeper cracks splintering my heart and a heavier burden of guilt on my soul. The outside campus of the institution stood in stark contrast to the composition of the halls and rooms within. My mom, having always been more connected to nature than any other realm, would walk with me over the grounds and show me her favorite places to sit in respite. A thermal creek ran through the property and she would linger there with her feet soaking in the warm, healing ripples.

When we returned to the facility where she resided, where there were a cafeteria and some common spaces, it felt void of any comfort—sterile—though I recognized the attempts to make it otherwise in the choice of couches, throw pillows, and curtains with which they adorned the lounge. Mom withdrew into herself the moment we stepped inside and became a vacant body, nothing of her soul present in these surroundings. We were both crushed.

Oakley was there with me when I stopped by the house to check on my mother before we went out dancing, months later. Mom had been released and was back home with my brother. In the span of three months, and with the help of her genius-level IQ, she'd convinced the doctors she was of sound mind. That's one thing that's hard to account for with psychological analysis—one's intelligence. Though I insisted I didn't feel she was yet herself, highly trained psychologists believed otherwise and sent her home. I guess a twenty-year-old (I'd just had a birthday) who'd spent her whole life with the patient wouldn't have much value to offer to such a discussion.

How could I navigate such decisions for the one person in my life that was supposed to be my compass? Mothers are infallible. Mothers are steady and solid; they aren't allowed to crumble. Mothers... Mom... My mom... deep breath.

TWELVE

Joining in Motherhood

"*I* assure you, if I can do it, you can too," Beth said, offering much-needed solace in my time of worry. Although Nick and I had planned to get pregnant, it was still a lot to take in. How was I going to handle all that comes with being a mother? How was I going to learn the ways of mothering without my own mom here to show me? And, how on earth would I be able to keep a little one alive and healthy, when I felt like it was a crap shoot whether I could do so even for myself? Was I mature enough to take care of a baby? I mean, at twenty-seven I felt like there were a lot of bad decisions I might still need to explore.

"You'll be a great mom, Katie." Beth sang these words to me in her most soothing voice. "And, you have all of us to help. Seriously, if I've kept my boy alive for this long, you'll be great." To her voice she added a little gravel with this last statement.

Nine months later, I asked Ashley to be with us in the delivery room for JD's birth. She was there for the birth of both my babies. She had earned a place at my bedside, especially after encouraging me to get help with my postpartum depression while pregnant with Sammy. My first delivery was so graceful (if there was a globally known sarcasm font, I'd use it here) that Ashley plainly stated at some point during the action she didn't plan on doing any of this in her future. Without yet knowing it, she was a few weeks pregnant at that very moment. So, there was no need to grapple with the choice.

Ashley got to see more of me that day than I've seen of myself. It was her choice to ask the doctor so many questions about what he was doing down there. Who knew Unicorns were so inquisitive? Every stitch and the reasoning behind it were given due explanation. "This is so interesting," she excitedly stated. "You should look at what he's doing down here." Nope—I'll pass.

Beth, her mom, and Lynn all joined Ashley and our family in the celebration of our first tiny baby boy at the hospital shortly after he was born. Beth's mom, Sarah, sat on the edge of my bed. The bleached white blankets were draped over my legs and the plastic hospital crib lay empty apart from one tiny blue pacifier. She held JD with tears running down her cheeks. He was swaddled comfortably in his colorful blanket, the white spots of a freshly-born face adorning his nose. He fluttered his eyelids and the corner of his mouth curved upward in his slumber.

My mom was no longer with us and did not get the opportunity to gently swaddle our baby boy, or gaze upon his innocent cherub face. Celebration and grief can be closely intertwined; Sarah grieved for me, even while reveling in the moment. She held him to her chest, followed the curve of his face delicately with a fingertip, and kissed his nose. She inhaled deeply the scent of blessing. I felt the warmth of overwhelming empathy and intimacy embrace me and our little one, as if my own mother were channeling her energy through Sarah. I was overcome by the undeniable recognition that a day I feared would be shadowed by a void no one could possibly fill was overflowing with a love I could never have anticipated.

My husband gingerly opened the hospital room door—after shakily, and inaccurately, completing the birth certificate for "Sandy" instead of Samuel—to a mist of tears and radiating estrogen. His smile grew wide and he shook his head in both question and endearment. He's never been one to understand all this 'woman' stuff, but he's always been genuine in his enjoyment of all that women are made of.

In true dramatic fashion, Beth gave me a sly and jealous glance as she said to her mom, "Seriously? You didn't even cry when you held my son for the first time, your first grandson." Her green eyes glared in her mother's direction, then twinkled in mine. She pushed red curls away from her face with her hands, then crossed her arms with a "humph." The theatrical moment allowed us to break the spell cast by past generations and move to laughter.

I was invited to be with Ashley for the births of both her precious babes—Lander, now nine, and Rio, seven going on twenty-three. Ashley's deliveries left me wondering if there was anything she didn't do remarkably well. Her babies came out strong and bewitching, just like their parents. Actually, that's not really true for Ashley's second child. Her little girl, Rio, came out purple and pissed. I don't know that I've heard a brand-new baby scream with such determination.

My cup overflowed with the joy of being a present witness and able to care for Ashley through the early hours and days of getting acquainted with her itty-bitty humans. It was such a gift to hear their first breaths, even if they were record-breakingly loud. They now call me Auntie Katie.

Throughout the years, twelve babies have been born to the six of us. For some, nothing was quite as consoling as a best friend sliding into the tub behind her, brushing and braiding her hair while labor progressed. For both mother and friend to feel at ease with each other is primal and everlasting.

Generations upon generations of women have come together in this way, driven by intuition to gather for the births of babies, drawing closer when the weather turned or the moon waxed to its fullest glory, to buttress one another. They knew the tidal power of the moon spilled forth and brought women into the trance of labor. Women, naked and baring themselves to each other, trusted their innate mammalian wisdom to bring new life into the arms of the women of their tribes. Our posse has chosen to celebrate this rite of passage, being present at the births of our little ones, helping to welcome babies into our collective family.

These wonderous segues into our chapters of motherhood were far removed from the clamoring and clawing by which I transitioned to adulthood. That passage was brutal.

THIRTEEN

A Hearth to Return to

The thing with coming of age is one might not be ready. In my case, the embers of angst started to smolder when I called the authorities for help with my mom, which burst into imminent flames. Set against an increasingly heartbreaking and complicated backdrop, my life was primed to either burn down or burn bright. Ready or not, my journey was set, and then precisely marked by one smoke-filled week.

On Day One, we said a final goodbye to Mom. Mom died the winter before, and this day was reserved to spread her ashes. From that day, my memories are not of people or conversations. I know there were a handful of friends with us, Matt and me. Luke was unable to join us; he was deployed with the army at the time. Beyond that, the memories I carry reflect only the surroundings and sensations of the day, as if my heart and soul took over, setting my actions and words to autopilot.

It was June 21, summer solstice. Mom loved to celebrate the longest day of the year. It was a fitting day to tread into the mountains to a place that held her heart. Driving into the canyon, I cradled the urn in my lap while Matt drove. I traced the intricate gold etchings around the neck of the black metal vessel shaped somewhat like a Russian doll. Flickering from in between the pine trees' shadows as they whizzed by, the sun spilled off the gold etchings in my hands and sent shards of light dancing.

As we got out of the cars and started up the trail, the trees parted and a meadow opened its arms to us. At the head of the meadow, the creek winded past and got wide at the turn. I saw my mom bent over the boulders on the curve of the bend, laughing and splashing us—three small children giggling and wet with wonder. My only memory of us here with her, came to me in a ripple of emotion.

With each step up the trail, the back and forth turns of the switchbacks, my chest grew heavier with the weight of saying goodbye. We passed beside light-green buds of spring, pine, the sweet trace of wild roses on the air, and rich periwinkle lupine scattered throughout the grassy clearings. We moved into the forest where the trees held us close. When we reached the end of the trail, and Mom's favorite waterfall, my eyes turned to the sky. The silhouettes of the trees spired, circular, pointing to the center. Our company came in close, shoulder to shoulder, hand in hand, in a reverent hush.

With a deep breath, I looked to Matt and we stepped down the steep decline of several boulders to get to the mouth of the waterfall. Just he and I, standing on the top of the cliff. As we unwrapped the plastic, my fingers fumbled. The breath created by the moving water sent the first few ashes sprinting to coalesce. I lowered my hands, holding gently the remains of my mom and her memories, to the lips of the current and sent Mom dancing down the crisp, clean waters of the place that held her heart for years. The stream echoed her song—one I still hear every time I visit her memory there.

Just before we left, Matt climbed a larch tree and placed Mom's favorite windchime on the lowest hanging branch, the needles soft and tender in their juvenile growth. Stoic and sullen, I turned and led us back down the hill without a word. The chimes rang in my ears, dancing with the whisper of the waterfall, barely audible as my body took over. Heel to toe, step by step I descended, with an empty urn in my arms and a part of my spirit severed. The sun slanted through the trees and blinded my view as it glinted off my tears.

Day One ended with an amicable breakup spurred by my then-boyfriend's decision to step away. Andrew had been kind and present in the year prior, so unlike other bad relational choices I'd made, but he was markedly absent from the memorial of sorts. I called Andrew when I got home to relay the beauty and blight of the experience. We moved away from that conversation and found a moment to finally express what we'd felt for too long. We'd reached the culmination of our passionate kinship. I was too broken to love him, to trust him, to bring joy to his world.

Day Two went missing entirely; grief is a thief that way. On Day Three, I turned over my husky dog, Shya, to new parents. She was Mom's dog. I inherited her after Mom died, but I was moving into an apartment where I couldn't have her. I said goodbye to Shya and my roommates on the same day and moved, without knowing any of the new housemates. On Days Four and Five, I slogged through the blurred transition that follows separation. Day Six was the day to register for a new semester at college. I changed my major from livestock management to English teaching—two loves, two opposing directions.

How was it I made my return from such devastation? Was I alone in pulling myself back together and walking into a new way of life? Not hardly. As is the way evidenced by cultures nearly since the beginning of civilization, I was ushered into the garments of my new existence by my elders. Members of my given and collected family, with arthritic hands that had stitched together textiles of experience for decades, disrobed me of my stained linens and washed me clean. I was offered the comfort of fresh cotton with which to dry myself before donning the serenity of silk.

As I crossed the threshold into my new existence, my friends were there waiting to join me on a new journey. I was no longer a child. My caramel eyes met theirs with an increased depth of perspective, the ever-present flecks of gold now accentuated by the underlying umber of woeful understanding.

FOURTEEN

Matriarchs

My mother's history of being one of the most vibrant examples of creating community among women, and building collective family, is shared within our posse. I've taken her lead and surrounded myself with women who embody the spirit of these things I hold most dear, helping me feel as close to her as is possible in her absence. They set my heart alight with the essence of my mother's love. Burned to ashes in one moment, the embers of the remarkable woman who once was are fanned and ignited by living representations of her greatness, kindness, and joy. The posse stands beside me in the warmth of her memory.

With the passing of years, only a handful of people currently in my life knew my mom. A few find it uncomfortable to talk about her, even today. Not my girls. Lynn and Beth have many memories of her. Jax, Ashley, and Kenzie didn't know her. They do, however, encourage me to relive the remarkable stories I carry. They don't shy away from such conversations. The light of these memories replaces the darkness of others.

My mom was one of the most convivial people I knew. My friends remind me regularly of how inviting she was. Everyone came in and out of our home as if it were their own, never knocking. My dad remembers Mom saying her goal in life was to raise children, animals, and food. She was an amazing gardener and our meals overflowed with fresh-grown produce. Many more

children than just her own flourished and grew wildly in her presence because
of the energy she poured into them.

⁂

If you spent time around our house, you were cared for as Mom's own.
As the next generation, we too allow each other to help wrangle wild kids.
The posse join as families at barbeques and celebrations: children, husbands,
and significant others. The kids rambunctiously play together with the animals, tractors, and water balloons and have a great time. Someone always
ends up getting minor scrapes that require care and a couple bandages, offered
by whatever moms happen to be in the vicinity at the time of the incident. It
warms my heart, especially having someone else yell at my kids for being
crazy, running through the mud, or picking on that one rooster. It eases the
burden on us all when we join together in this way.

Twenty years after our own mothers opened this possibility in our hearts,
Beth and Lynn help me remember mine and all she offered us. Beth often
regales me with stories of time in our home. The story she tells most often is
of one particular night we were all together in our kitchen. Beth was entertaining as usual, and Mom was a more-than-willing audience member. For
some reason Beth had placed a slice of bread on each cheek, moved them
forward and back like gills, and made a fish face with her lips. That was all it
took to get us laughing so hard we couldn't stop. Every time we tried to compose ourselves, we would burst out loud again and couldn't even look at each
other.

Beth shares this story often, and for what I believe is a dual purpose. We
both find a great measure of pride in knowing each other so well and for so
long. Such a story is evidence of our long-standing friendship. On a deeper
level, though, this is a story of Beth's knowing, of knowing me, but more so
of being a recipient of the immense gift of knowing Mom. We share these
gifts of experience; tender them for joy.

The intergenerational matriarchal care and validation that has inspired
me to move through pain and cultivate my own family has come from a collective of women: the posse as well as dear surrogate moms. Many nights of
stripping back the layers of my history, revealing the naked truths about my

life to my friends, have illuminated the depth of inspiration I've received throughout the years.

* *

I have an affinity for independent, strong, and intelligent women. This is not only true of my Wax Night compatriots, but also includes other barnstorming, mountain-climbing, high-flying, adventurous women in midlife and beyond who are vibrant and full of energy. I have incredible role models in my life whom I esteem. If my girls are the scaffolding of my life, these women are the soaring mountains and the dazzling sun toward which this scaffolding stretches. The gratitude I feel for the older women who inspire me resonates at a much different frequency.

Mary Beth, MB for short, is one of these women. With full measure of my childhood, I recognize that even though I experienced a chasm of loneliness, there were small spheres of safety that shielded me from time to time. MB came into the pages of my story when I was in grade school. This energized woman, with light complexion, dark hair, and a smile that dances in your memory for days, was my dad's partner at the time. She lived with my dad and me for quite a few years. She taught me lessons, of course, as one would any child: eat healthy, dress warmly, get exercise, sit up straight, brush your teeth well.

These lessons, though certainly valuable, are not the ones I carry with me to this day. What I carry in my heart are the truths she taught me with caring, and her posture and approach to living. Rites of passage aren't always isolated events, separate from the daily. Sometimes the transition from child to young woman, from despondent to directed, is encouraged by watching our ideals personified. MB, through watching her in action, taught me how to value myself as much as she did and showed me I was remarkable and worth loving... to the ends of the earth.

During my teenage years, there were many people in my life who stated the importance of having a foundation of high self-esteem. MB showed me. She carried within herself a confidence that came from taking the time to know and trust her own worth. She strategically, day by day, little by little, built this foundation with conscientious effort and close attention. No lesson compares to witnessing firsthand the radiance of a woman who truly values herself.

MB intentionally built physical toughness with her everyday endeavors. Though her frame was small, she exhibited much strength. She chose jobs that took muscle: white-water rafting guide and guiding for an outfitter in the wilderness on horseback. These jobs fulfilled her craving to be outdoors and proved she was capable and driven. She hefted eighteen-foot rafts onto trailers, four stacked on top of one another, for transport to and from the river. She packed and unpacked a full kitchen each day of the ten to fifteen-day trips in the Bob Marshall wilderness to feed guests, handling both the heavy leather bundles off the backs of the mules and the mules themselves with great strength and care. She knew the value of her own hard work in a posture of humility.

Not only was I witness to the strength of character within her but she also bestowed upon me grace and kindness to help build such within myself. MB, with short dark hair, now peppered with grey, and eyes that look upon the world with such delicate promise, saw through my strong outer presentation and found the small young woman inside that yearned for worth, value, something to bring her gaze up from the ground in order to walk a little taller. MB helped me to see the glimmering places within me, shed light upon the elements of myself that were remarkable.

We shared a love for horses. They offered solace and understanding in a way more dynamic than anything else. Horses, in combination with the wild outdoors, were the perfect pairing with which to nourish our souls. MB worked as the camp cook for a ranch that gave guided horse pack trips into the wilderness. These were trips that included ten or more days in the mountains with clients that craved such an experience. She invited me to help in the kitchen in exchange for being able to tag along. In this, she secured for me a dream that would leave me awestruck.

For ten days, I spent each day swaying in the saddle with the motion of Little Joe—the horse beneath me—listening to the clack and tramp of his hooves landing on gravel, soil, and grasses on the trail and the creak of the leather saddle. Both the motion and the sounds seemed to echo the timing of my heartbeat, connecting my energy with his. My eyes danced from one brilliant gleaming mountaintop to the next, the rugged peaks outlined in silhouette as the sun thrust from behind them his brilliant rays of light. Each evening, guests and guides gathered together and listened to cowboy stories around a crackling campfire, the sound of the cowboy's voice rugged and rich, smoke clinging to our clothes to later dull our senses to sleep with its sooty and earthy smell. Each night we were ushered into dreams by the gentle winds as they sang through the tops of the trees, nestled under dazzling stars.

Watching MB as her eyes wandered over every detail of this amazing landscape, her face expressing the purest delight and wonderment, inspired us all to slow down and treasure the gifts before us. There was no question as to the depth of her feelings for this place, for this team of horses, for the family she made in the cowboys with which she worked. It was as though her gratitude and astonishment became words etched on her lips, perceived through the subconscious contemplation of her gaze and the flicker in her eyes.

Though the experience of the horses and the landscape was magical, it was MB's encouragement of my inner strength that elevated this trip to a level I didn't know possible. She saluted the work ethic I demonstrated on those long days, rising early in the morning to prepare western omelets and toast for the guests, lowering myself from the saddle at the end of the day's miles to then move forward with setting up the kitchen. I could see the unmistakable welling of pride in her eyes as she watched me start water to boil and prepare vegetables, watching the guests while my hands washed over pans in the cold rinse water, as they sat mesmerized by the reddish alpenglow on the summits of the mountains just after sunset.

Nothing made the excitement and wonder of the trip pale, not even the accident that occurred on day eight of the ten-day trip. During an exquisite day in the mountains, we gazed down from the top of the Chinese Wall, a fault line that projects hundreds of feet of sheer cliff. We sat upon the edge and marveled at the majesty of such a natural formation, felt small and wondrous looking down upon the minute landscape below. The Swainson's thrush sang its crescendo, the treetops danced with sun-kissed gold, and both guides and guests were enveloped in the wonder of the land. This is where I've always felt the closest to God. Spirituality seems to be infused in such a work of grandeur.

After mounting our horses, we plodded down the trail, making our way off the mountain to our camp. We rounded a hillside, entered a small meadow rippling with waves of grass coaxed by a gentle wind, and stumbled upon a black bear. Horses do not like bears. They don't like the smell, sound, or sight of them. What do you do when you encounter a bear while on horseback? You keep moving.

Or, in this case, as the bear was a little way off the trail and a small one, you allow the guests who've flown in from all around the nation to sit and watch in the kind of fear and wonder that elicits an indescribable excitement. All is well and good until you give your trusty steed a gentle nudge forward, releasing the tension and anxiety he has built up in his muscles from the moments of quiet trepidation within which he has been standing, and you end up getting stomped by said trusty steed. Some cowboy I am.

After such a stomping, MB showed admiration for the strength it took to rise out of my tent the next morning and go about fulfilling my obligations, chest still throbbing and eyes darkening to black from the crushing blows of his hooves. She commended me for the grit it took to get back in the saddle and ride out, hurting like I was. She celebrated all these things I would not have thought remarkable about myself. MB loved every piece of me and held up those pieces before me in her steady hands, one by one, until I saw them too reflected in my image. Today I still reach for the examples she showed me and walk my journey with them clutched tightly to my chest. She proved to me, beyond reasonable doubt, that I had value and strength.

MB continues to be a foundation of fortitude in my life. I call upon her often, especially as a mother myself.

FIFTEEN

The Round Table

As women and mothers, we bare more than our legs to one another. After years of shared time and momentous events, we've been blessed with relationships deep enough to safely bare our souls. It's only natural then that we deliberate over motherhood around the table at Wax Night. It is here we're afforded the opportunity to express our frustrations, fears, triumphs, failures, and ongoing efforts regarding our children. Tonight, is no exception.

Lynn has just used the clippers to trim her nether regions and has now assumed the position on the waxing mat, the opaque milky-mint stone of her necklace slightly off kilter as it rests along her collar bone. She reaches with her fingertips to move it to center. Beth is taking a turn being the waxer for a change. Lynn is patient when she coaches us. Both Beth and I have taken turns waxing our fearless aesthetician, Lynn. We're learning the tricks of the trade and they're not for the faint of heart.

The right wax helps us rookies do a better job—one we tried was much too sticky to be successful, one too thin for proper application. We finally found one that works well. It's a pale purple color and has a subtle yet soothing scent, which does little to offset the nature of its use, truth be told.

One of the things I always forget, but Lynn is keenly aware to remind me, is that baby powder goes on the skin first. If you forget, you're in for an uncomfortable result. The baby powder allows the wax to strip the hair, but not the skin. Don't forget the baby powder.

Beth dusts Lynn with talc, smooths it off with a cotton ball, grabs a tongue depressor (that's what the wooden waxing sticks look like to me) and sets to work. She executes one thin swipe of wax, followed by a strip of waxing paper applied with deliberate weight onto the area, and then focuses a generous amount of energy on ripping the strip off in just the right direction while pressing firmly on the adjacent skin.

As Beth continues her work, Jax sets the stage for a whole different level of reveal. "OK, are you listening? Are you all ready for this?" she asks with excitement in her voice. "Daisy went on a date. A boy asked, and she said yes."

"Wait, our little Daisy?"

"Yes. And, it went well," she says, pushing her toolkit/purse aside while reaching for a dish with lime wedges to squeeze into her gin. "I hounded her before the date about how he asked, what she thought. I think she appreciates my relentless inquisitions about, well, everything." In spite of Jax's comedic overstating, she's the type of mother who expects her daughter to talk and be honest. As a single mom, parenting's exclusively up to her, and I'm always impressed at how open and honest Jax is, yet still considerate of the privacy a teenage girl no doubt craves.

"I'm glad Daisy is shy about boys," Lynn says from the kitchen floor, in earnest. Beth pushes back her copper bangs and whips off another quick strip of wax.

"I'm relieved she hasn't yet followed in our footsteps," I say from my seat at the table, cringing at Lynn's current predicament and the thought of our children doing some of the stupid stuff we did. We weren't shy about boys— well most of us weren't. Lynn was the exception. She embraced books. They were the only things accompanying her to bed. I, however, lettered in flirtation my senior year and Beth held a self-taught doctorate in dating—what she considered advanced placement classes. Ashley was living with her boy-friend-now-husband before she even graduated high school.

All these things seemed elevated goals to us when we were Daisy's age. We embraced our pursuits and thought highly of our efforts, even looked with pride upon ourselves for the accomplishments we now view as adequately horrifying possibilities through the lens of motherhood and how they apply to our own children.

Kenzie flips through photos on her phone and tugs the shoulder of her wrap sweater back into place. She listens but can't help interjecting from where she relaxes in the corner seat at the table. Kenzie doesn't get waxed, so she always sits out of the way of all the commotion. She's also the most physically conservative of us all, a little prudish, if I must say so. She and Jax are the least likely to bare themselves for a wax, or to glance at our naked bottom halves in the kitchen. Kenzie's seat in the corner serves her well. She hands us snacks from her side of the table and serves up wisdom when it comes. She's less reserved in her nature as a mother, however.

"That's why I'm open with my children about sex and relationships, even though they're still young." She sets her face in a motherly scowl. "I say, 'Wrap it up. If you don't, it could kill you.'" When we all stop and look, she throws her hands up beside her shoulders, palms both facing up, as if to say "what?"

"It's crazy out there. I explain all the different things that can go wrong; I'm not above scaring 'em to help 'em understand the seriousness of their choices."

"I mean...," I take a sip of my Huckleberry vodka and soda, "I know there are certain circumstances that could, in fact, kill you when it comes to unprotected sex, but really, Kenz?" I ask. I tend to be less dramatic in the delivery of information to my boys.

"Oh, don't judge," Beth chimes in (a mother of a fifteen-year-old boy) while grabbing the tweezers to pluck a couple rogue hairs from Lynn's landing strip. Her green eyes lock on the rest of us, "When ten-year-old Phillip had the audacity to tell me for the first time that he didn't want to give me a kiss when I dropped him off at school, I guilted him. 'What if I died in a car accident on my way to work today and the last thing you remember is not kissing me goodbye? You are never too old to kiss your mother.' To this day, he gives me a kiss every morning when I drop him off."

Lynn glares up at Beth from between her legs, "Only because your child is such a sympathetic and gentle soul, which is why I can't believe you threatened him with death to get a kiss. You're so dramatic." She parents along the same lines I do. We're allowed our own parenting opinions, and the space to disagree. Beth rips a strip from Lynn's thigh in repayment, nonetheless, for good measure.

As Lynn moves her legs to the upright position, for better Brazilian waxing access, she laments, "It's hard to parent. I've done all I can think to do. Still, my daughter—at the same age—acts the polar opposite of Daisy." She lets go of one leg and rubs a hand across her face, as if trying to wipe away the fatigue. "What's wrong with me? What's wrong with Cara? I know each kid has a different personality and perspective, but how can they end up making such different decisions?"

Lynn's daughter and Jax's daughter have such opposing innate personalities that this really isn't a fair comparison. Lynn's daughter is outgoing, stupidly dependent upon her friends and their opinions, and stubborn. And smart. Cara is too intelligent for her own good. She's been sneaking out, stealing, smoking, driving without a license, and throwing parties at her dad's house when he's gone, along with making a multitude of other troubling choices. Though she's been put on probation and brought in on several occasions by law enforcement, none of the consequences have slowed the momentum of her behavior.

"You really have tried everything to get her to quit making such bad choices. The truth is, each decision you've made has been with such love in your heart, no matter how furious you've felt. You haven't given up. You've taken the hard route that encourages her to learn and grow. I can't say I'd be strong enough to do that," I say and pass by on the way to get some water. I lean down to mess her hair and bring my hand to rest on her shoulder.

Ashley, tonight wearing jeans formerly covered in sawdust, now with just hints of work dusting the creases, piggybacks on that thought as she reaches across the table for a chip and scrapes the side of the guacamole bowl, "You've put all the tools she needs within her reach. She has to choose to use them."

I make eye contact with Ashley and nod in agreement. I continue, with a soft tone, "If I were in the same situation, would you question my judgment and ability to parent? Would you get frustrated with me for not being able to fix these problems?"

"Of course not," Lynn whispers as she lets out a breath and relaxes her shoulders into the waxing mat.

"Well, then, give yourself extra measures of grace right now. You're doing all you can."

I pick through the mixed nuts to find the Brazil nut hiding at the bottom of the dish. I find that one of the best bits of advice I receive from these women is being kinder to myself, which in turn includes an understanding that parenting is arduous for even the most prepared and resourceful parent. I've known astoundingly successful businesswomen who never appear to be plagued by doubt about their ability at work but suffer crushing uncertainty when making decisions in the realm of parenting. Why do we allow ourselves to feel as though every single decision our children make is dictated by our ability to parent and our success in doing so, for the rest of their lives? We end up thinking, *If I don't handle this correctly, he may never know the value of hard work*, or *If I can't get a handle on her behavior now, how will she ever be successful as an adult?* I think we can all benefit from treating ourselves with kindness and grace as mothers.

"Want to know what my son learned today?" I ask as I laugh to myself.

"Do tell."

"We went to eat at the café and the owner has a sign by the door. Why is it new readers spot anything to read in their midst? Well, the sign read 'Beware of pick pockets and loose women.' I've never noticed it before. Not until Sammy asked, 'Mom, what are loose women?'"

"Oh, man. That's amazing," Beth says as she laughs.

"I had to ask him where he heard that and he pointed to the sign. At that moment, Chris, the owner, walked by. I've known him for years now. I called him over and told him Sammy had a question."

"No you didn't," Ashley interjected with her eyes bright with anticipation.

"Sure did. The best part is that he came here from Switzerland and has a thick accent. He squirmed and said, 'I don't know English very well. I don't know what that word means,' which is total crap. He came back a few minutes later, looked at Sammy, and said, 'OK, I have an answer. Loose women are the ones you have fun with.'"

I start laughing and have to pull myself together before finishing the story. "To which Sammy replied, with much joy evident in his tone and wide smile, 'So, Mom's a loose woman?'"

The girls' laughter expands the room and Kenzie blushes a bit.

"I had to set Sammy straight and actually tell him it wasn't a kind thing to say to someone. That I would explain why when he was a little older, but loose women were ones that had a lot of sex with lots of different men. Not his mom."

"Definitely not his mom," Lynn acknowledges with a glance my way. She knows my sex drive has never been much to brag about.

"If sex drive had a speed limit, yours would be a school zone," Jax interjects.

"And Lynn's and Ashley's, the Autobahn?" I counter. "What can I say. Some women just drive faster than others." Lynn and Ashley both beam with what we truly consider a compliment. A healthy sex drive is something we all aspire to.

As this discussion comes to a close, Beth works on the finishing touches of Lynn's Brazilian wax, the kind where one gets the vaginal lips and behind waxed, as well as the bikini line and along the thighs. This is the preference of all of those that wax here. Beth, however, is a rookie as the waxer. This becomes overtly evident to us all in very short order.

"What are you doing???" Lynn says in the elevated tone she reserves for desperate and panicked occasions. "Don't wax that. I need it!"

"That's my finger, Carolynn, not wax," Beth bellows to compete with Lynn's tone. "It's fine. I know the importance of leaving your sexy parts intact. Relax, it's just my finger," she reiterates in reassurance.

"Don't rip off my...," Lynn plainly states, clapping a hand over the cleft between her thighs for good measure.

The four of us at the table howl with laughter. Ashley chokes out that she's going to pee her pants as she crosses her legs just in case. Jax and I wipe tears from our eyes, unable to respond. Kenzie hollers in half fear for Lynn and half uncontrollable giggling, "Beth, what the hell are you doing? Stop." Lynn's holding her tummy, she's laughing so hard, and all of our cheeks and sides start to hurt so good.

Part Three

SIXTEEN

Girls Just Want to Have Fun

*M*y little boys have grown accustomed to my girls' nights and revel in that time with only their dad. These are the nights Nick makes up the pullout couch and all three of them camp in the living room together. They enjoy a movie and popcorn and the change of management styles with their dad. They usually usher me out of the house even before my intended departure, encouraging the start to an evening full of special moments for us all.

One week each year, in particular, the posse gets together for a full weekend of reverie. El Wencho plays at our favorite place two or three times a year. This get-together happens to be one of the best times to have recently waxed our bikini lines, even if only a select few of us would be caught dead in a bikini at this juncture in our lives. Yes, our perfectly sculpted Ashley, with her tan skin and narrow waistline, is one of those fearless few.

We have hot springs in Montana, pools of steaming water that draw up from the ground, heated by thermal activity in our volcanic environment. God's water, nature's outdoor jacuzzi tubs with healing natural minerals brought forth from the earth. One location was developed at the turn of the century as a resort destination. It's been improved since then to accommodate lodging, food, a spa, and venues for entertainment and adventure, including an old cowboy bar with worn wooden floors and nicotine so deeply engrained in the walls, it counts as second-hand smoking just to breathe in there.

The resort is huddled in an awe-inspiring setting in the vicinity of Yellowstone National Park with all its majesty, life, and spirit wrapped up against a jagged and monumental mountain range. A winding back-road leads into the mouth of these mountains and drops into the heart of a remarkably beautiful place. On each side of the road is the shared company of grazing horses in the pastures that hug the elevating landscape. Rough-sawn peaks tower over this spot of respite and the sun filters down through the steam of the hot springs, revealing rainbows and rippling glimmers of light. Herein sits the old hotel with its rustic charm and delightful, beautifully crafted rooms. The soul of the mountains seems to reverberate in the structures, the animals found here, and in the swaying of the grasslands, an energized little microcosm of activity and one of our all-time favorite places.

If you're not from around here, though, it's not worth seeing. Trust me on this. Stay where you are. This place is 'rustic' and 'old' and you wouldn't want to endure it.

During these weekends away, we all gather into several rooms or one big cabin. We unpack our bed rolls and all claim a spot where we will surrender to the night after a day of mischief. We round up the ingredients needed to prepare a meal as the sustenance to energize our evening of soaking, singing, dancing, and raucous conversation.

Tonight, we congregate in the kitchen of the cabin and each contribute to the gastro-pub creation. I brought the tortillas, others the rest of the fixings for our tacos. We brown the burger, spread all the toppings out on the counter, and warm the crispy taco shells in the oven by placing them upside down so they hang on the racks, broiling them for a minute. Jalapeños are doled out as delegated, and only to those wanting to get spicy. Some of us make burritos, some nachos. We sit around the coffee table, share glasses of wine, and unravel ourselves from the constraints of our normal daily routines. We settle into the energy of friendship and the celebration of our time together.

After the meal, we change into our swimsuits. Lynn, while putting on hers, has a tidbit to voice. "I told my boyfriend I might stop waxing for a while. He said that was just fine, if I still kept it up, still use clippers to keep things maintained. He doesn't want a mustache down there. That's where he draws the line."

"A mustache?" Kenzie questions, eyes raising to the right as the lines draw between her brows. Ashley's more than happy to oblige an explanation.

"Happens in no time at all. When my hair gets too long it looks like I have a little dude wearing a mask. Each side has hairs bushing out." She's holding her hands over her bikini line, twisting her fingers in the air as if waxing her imaginary mustache into the globally recognized Western style. "That's why I shave so often."

We giggle and throw on the fluffy robes that hang behind the bathroom doors and make our way down to the pools for some relaxation. We dip our feet into the soothing water, and it ripples in response. The water seems to wash away our daily sins and consecrates us, preparing us for a new start. Some of us spend a bit of time in the quiet hot water, alone, as to enjoy a seldom-found moment of solitude.

When we are gathered here during a winter weekend, the hot springs take on a much different tenor than in summertime. On these cold and snowy days, I can hardly see across the pool as the warmth of the water produces a cloud of thick steam. I'm encouraged by the embrace of the weather to sink deep into the water.

For me, these moments are the best of both worlds. I'm allowed to sit and relax in solitude all the while being serenaded by the melody of my dearest friends' laughter and conversation. Rejuvenation at its most primitive, as if even the solar system is persuading our worries to dispel. The early-evening moon is growing larger as we sit below it, the stars appearing one at a time to join our endeavors when the breeze briefly sweeps the steam aside in a whirl to reveal them. Our time in the pool comes to an end when we move from relaxed to the start of renewed promise by a night of entertainment. We get excited for adventure and move on to phase three.

As we get gussied up to listen and dance to the band, we fall into a familiar rhythm and take turns primping. One of us changes into her outfit while another lies on the bed chatting and offering support for the wardrobe of choice. We have the music cranked and Jax belts out the lyrics with expert enthusiasm. We each help button this and curl that. "Can I use your lipstick?" "Ooh, that smells amazing. Can I have a spritz of that on my hair?" "Do these pants look ok?" "Is this shirt showing too much cleavage?" By the way, the answer to all is yes, but the last question is always, "No!" We're all done around the same time... except for Jax. We're always waiting on Jax. Perfection takes time.

Any night out starts with Jax's careful preparation. Tonight, she's chosen the black crushed-velvet top that shows off her shoulders coupled with a plunging neckline. She adds to this a flowing skirt and large sparkly earrings that catch the light as they dangle just above her shoulders, and then spends considerable time perfecting the artwork that is her makeup: smoldering eyes, perfectly crafted brows, seductive lip color, and the kind of contouring that makes the movie star makeup artists cringe at their own work. When all is said and done, she comes away looking and smelling like a million dollars. I don't know what combination of miracles she uses, but she smells better than anyone I've met: delicious and uniquely her.

The whole time Jax compiles this elegant and refined conduit for her soul, she carries on in tawdry conversation. Her curse words bounce off of the walls, from the room, all the way down the hall to the living room. "Can't there be more than two outlets in a room in this contemptible place?"

"What's your problem?" Kenzie asks in earnest. "Do I need to come in there and do your hair?"

"No, damn it! They really should accommodate those of us who strive for an elevated presentation with the means necessary to execute such an endeavor."

Beth walks into the room and lies on the bed beside where Jax is attempting to primp, her copper hair spilling over the pillow, "You are fine. Settle down," she says, knowing that telling Jax to settle down is like hissing at a honey badger.

"You shut it. You know nothing of my struggles." And, with a thick accent resembling what you might hear in the Bronx, she adds, "You don't know me! You don't know what it's like!" snapping her fingers from side to side and jutting her chin from left to right to exemplify as much sass as she can.

"You look amazing. Let's go," says Ashley tapping a rhythm with her boot. It takes Ashley about four minutes to look incredible, and she's not one who waits well.

"Don't be daft! It takes time to look this good. And you will sit here and enjoy waiting as I craft this masterpiece."

This kind of formidable confidence has always amazed me. I don't actually think it goes to the depth of her being, but she presents it better than anyone I know.

"Come to think of it, all this work is making me hungry," she simply states waltzing into the kitchen where we're all visiting, waiting for her to finish. She grabs a banana from the cooler, peals it halfway, and brings it up to her mouth.

"Whatcha gonna do with that, Jax?" Beth says with a salacious undertone to her voice.

A smirk spreads across Jax's face. "Why, Beth. You have seemingly taken a most unladylike turn toward the depraved and licentious with such a comment," she pauses to inspect her banana. "I like it!"

"OK, Lynn, can you look up the word 'licentious' for the rest of us?" Kenzie chimes in. "Actually, scratch that. Who actually knows how to spell? We all know it isn't Lynn."

This garners a wave of laughter, especially from Lynn. One of the endearing things about Lynn is she spells everything phonetically. Everything. And, depending on how she's always pronounced a word, it may be anything but accurate. Even her autocorrect cannot figure out what word she's trying to use when she types 'melk.'

"If we can't spell it and don't know what it means, are we still friends, Jax?" I ask in jest.

"Nope! I'll have nothing more to do with you," she responds, turns on her heels, and walks back into the room to finish the sculpting and her banana.

When we finally do make it down to our old friend, the local tavern, we commence our usual boisterous evening listening to the band. We've become experts in balancing the necessity to remain responsible and accountable to our families, with advocating for the most tremendous time possible. Some of us drink, others don't. Some of us dance, others don't. All of us chat, connect, unwind, and play... with gusto.

As we meander through the night, Jax continues to be the comedic relief in any number of ways, often engaging laughter so rousing our stomachs are sore the next day—a side effect we don't mind. We spend hours having fun before deciding to call it a night and head back to our cabin.

We cap off the night by dressing down, pulling up our hair, washing our faces, and settling in. After donning comfortable nighttime attire, we gather again in the living room for a last bout of time together, allowing a deeper dive into conversation. We snuggle in, comforted by one another's company. If the weather is warm enough, lying out on the lush green grass and looking up at the expansive, twinkling sky is a must. Sometimes we lie out there for hours. It's amazing to me the difference in depth of connection when out in this beautiful setting. It's as if our souls become as open as the world around us.

After hours together, and staying up way too late, we make our way to our beds, strip down into our lacey bras and panties, grab our feather pillows, and....

Not quite. We've never had a pillow fight... not yet, anyway.

SEVENTEEN

Time to Come Clean

The next day, as I wake, I'm drawn to the winter landscape framed by the window in my room. The clouds plunge over the snow-capped mountains, pushed down by the winds as if cascading waterfalls along the ravines carved decades ago. They spill over the valley, enveloping it with the high pressure of a storm system. Something in my heart tugs and reminds me today is the anniversary of my mom's death: January 21.

I pull out my phone and search for the picture of her and me when I was a baby, both of us in the bathtub, brimming with playfulness. I took a picture of this picture with my phone so I can gaze upon it whenever I feel the need. The charcoal marble tile and the clawfoot tub give away the era during which someone made this moment everlasting. I cherish the way it captures my mom's smile. I can feel it in my heart even after her passing. I select the picture and send it to my little brother, Luke, now stationed in Texas at Ft. Hood. He and I share the intimacy of this deep loss, a solidarity formed by both of us witnessing the demise of our mother with our own eyes, feeling it deep within our hearts. Now, we are each other's citadel.

One of the things I embrace wholeheartedly about a weekend at the hot springs is that I can sleep in. I put my phone down, glance at the time, and decide to allow myself to crawl back under my blankets. The feather pillows embrace me as I shed tears of latent grief and fall back into a sleep dictated by sadness. It's been nearly twenty years since family and friends gathered on top of a mountain similar to this one, casting Mom's ashes down the falls. My tears exhaust me. Sleep restores some energy, but I still carry the burden of a weight greater than the blankets hugging tightly to my body.

After a time, I wake again and stretch the energy into my muscles as I enter into a wide yawn. With a swish of covers, my feet hit the floor and I pull back the heavy curtains to gaze out the window again. The landscape is leaden with snow, with the encumbrance of winter. I take my sweet time waking up. Finally, my tummy sounds the alarm to get moving. I pull on my swimsuit, then my sweatpants, then my "Sugar Momma" sweatshirt. El Wencho has a song called "Sugar Beets" and the sweatshirt is merchandise I purchased from them last night. The feel of the fabric was too soft to pass up. The comfort of its embrace is worth every penny this morning.

I meander down to the lobby of the hotel, grab a small bite to eat and a large cup of coffee loaded with cream and sugar. I only like coffee if it doesn't taste like coffee—merely a conduit for caffein and calories. I slouch into an oversized chair in front of the fireplace and enjoy the warmth of its blaze. I am unsure of how long I sit there, which is ideal for a day like this. I have nowhere to be and nothing on my schedule. The fire begins to radiate off my face, my clothing, a bit too warm. I strip off my sweatshirt but am unwilling to move from my seat. That would take too much energy. Instead, I stare into the flames as my cheeks flush with the heat.

I am roused from my vacant stare by a text on my phone. The rest of the girls are up and heading to the pool. It has started snowing lightly again, which makes the pools that much more inviting. The distraction of conversation and the support of my girls within reach are gifts on a difficult day of remembrance such as this. As soon as I set my phone down, it rings. I recognize the number—ah, my little bother! Yep, he's a bother some days. But, not today. Today's different.

I rise from my chair and my feet sound my elevation up the stairs toward my room.

I answer as I always do, "Hey, kid."

"Hey," the phone crackles. Wait... that's not phone static. That's the unmistakable sound of crushing grief. I recognize it in a split second. My feet stumble a bit on the final step to the second floor.

"Are you OK? What's going on?"

"I... I just...," he wrestles with even these words, before heaving back into uncontrollable sobs.

My chest is suddenly heavy with the weight of such sadness. I fumble with the key to unlock my room. "Just breathe, kid... just breathe. It's ok. It'll be ok. Just breathe."

I hear a couple stunted sobs catch in his throat and then a heavy exhale, "I just miss her. I wrote her a letter," he pauses. "But I have nowhere to send it."

I move to the bed, crossing my legs underneath me as I shift to the middle of the mattress. We sit in silence on the phone, each crying on each other's shoulders. "I know. It's a hard day. But I know she sees us through the clouds and shines her light down on us every day. She's proud of you. I know it."

I hear this grown man, this strong and fearless Army Staff Sergeant, with anguish strangling his every breath. I hold the phone close and try to lift him out of his emotions one small sentence at a time. Gradually, he's able to talk and share what he's going through.

I put a pillow behind my back and lean against the headboard. "You know, I wrote a letter the other day, too. I haven't finished it yet, but it was to you. I wanted to tell you how incredibly sorry I am for not caring for you the way I should have after mom died." Twenty years of burden flash through my limbs, a jolt, then a tremble. I didn't save our mom, and then I ran furiously, leaving Luke alone with the hellacious loss. He was young, alone, abandoned, orphaned.

I sit quiet with the weight of that statement. I've never before put this guilt into words. It has weighed heavy on my heart for all these years. I haven't been able to acknowledge this failure of mine. Not to anyone, hardly even to my own soul. "You were only sixteen. How could I have... have been so selfish in my own life?"

My body starts shivering with intensity now, my guilt bubbling up from the dark cavern in which it hid. I lie down on the bed and tears spill over my nose and onto my pillow. I clutch the blankets and pull them close to my chest. Maybe they will somehow soften the blow.

I continue, "I feel like I abandoned you. You didn't have anyone to lean on," I whisper.

Silence. Then, all of a sudden, Luke starts laughing. He starts with a bit of snarky, quiet laughter. I listen in absolute confusion. My attention is hijacked a moment by the fervor of short, quick strides in the hall. A passel of children bumble past on their way to the pool, their enthusiasm bouncing through the thin wooden door off the walls of my room.

Luke's initial chuckle then turns into a roar, a contagious one that encourages even me to want to join in. Yep, now he's laughing uncontrollably. I'm speechless, rising my chest from the bed, switching the phone from one ear to the other.

When he finally catches his breath he says, "Are you kidding me? You're kidding, right? We both knew your memory was bad, but this is unbelievable. Un-fucking-believable. Katie, that couldn't be farther from the truth! Have you even met yourself? You aren't capable of doing that."

"What? What do you mean? I'm so confused right now."

"Oh my God, Katie. Your memory's ridiculous. You were there for me more than I could've possibly asked for. Don't you remember, you came over almost every day to check on me? You paid my bills for months because I was so busted up I couldn't get out of bed and my legal fines so I could get into the army. You seriously couldn't have done more to support me. Unbelievable." Another short laugh and a pause. "You don't remember any of that?"

I'm having a hard time wrapping my brain around what he's saying. I've been carrying this ugly, gnawing guilt for twenty years, this deep-seated, putrid disgust for the fact that I wasn't strong enough to wrap my arms around my little brother when he was left with no one else. It's a vivid memory to me, the failure. Not a day has passed that I doubted the integrity of the mind that hammered this feeling into the darkness of my heart.

"I'm glad you didn't send me the letter," he says.

At this I laugh a little, and then a lot, and then I start to howl. What else can I do? *Unbelievable* is the right word. My memory is worthless, I knew that, but how could my mind have crafted such feelings and held them for so long when they were so far from the truth? I'm glad I didn't send that letter. Maybe I should have written it fifteen years ago and saved myself some grief?

Luke and I laugh so hard, we cry, and cry so hard, we laugh. We talk for a while longer and then he has to go back to duty. We exchange "I love you's" and I hang up the phone.

Now I definitely need a drink. I heft myself off the bed, take a deep breath, grab my money and my key, and head down to the pool. The girls are in the big pool when I arrive and wave me over. I don't think I'm yet sturdy enough to join them. I slip into the smaller, hotter pool. It isn't long before Beth and Ashley come to join me.

Ashley takes one look at me and asks, "What happened?" The concern grows on her face as my tears start up once again.

"I just got off the phone with my brother. It's a hard day for us. We had a really good talk, but it was a hard one," I start. I take a minute to think about what I'm about to say... admit... out loud... for the second time today.

"I felt so guilty. I told Luke how much I regretted not taking care of him after our mom died." Ashley and Beth sit beside me, just listening. The tears of release gently pool in the corners of my eyes, slipping down my cheeks. Ashley takes my wayward strands of hair and tucks them behind my ear, then brushes the tears from my cheeks with her thumb. Both their eyes glisten with empathy as Beth embraces me.

Then I start laughing again. The same bewilderment I felt shows on their faces. "But it wasn't true!" I sound out, my voice loud then cracking. "What I remembered wasn't true at all. I was there for him, he said. I did all I could, he said." This is all ludicrous.

The girls start to giggle with me. They shake their heads, undoubtedly recalling all the times they witnessed my memory failing me in the past.

"Alright girls. I need a minute. Give me a bit and I'll come join you."

As the girls swim away, I am left alone with my thoughts. I cry a little more, laugh a little more, and then I push myself under the water. I sink all the way to the bottom and sit there motionless, only moving with the gentle sway of the water. It's silent. I relax into the weightlessness the water affords. When I finally feel centered, I breach the surface and push my hair back with my fingers. The water cascades down my face, my shoulders, my arms. I open my eyes, take a deep, restorative breath, and lift my face to the sky. Laying my head back on the side of the pool, the snowflakes settle on my face, each flake an infinitesimally tiny, cold kiss lasting only milliseconds before warming to my skin. A thousand kisses caress my face, neck, and chest.

The rest of me relaxes into the warmth and weightlessness of the soothing water, a stark contrast to the feeling I had more than twenty years ago on the night my brother had called and said I needed to come check on Mom, said he was afraid for her. She was in bed when I arrived. My brother was right.... Could I have made a difference if I'd gotten there sooner?

EIGHTEEN

When I Needed You Most

The night Luke called me to come over, it was overtly evident Mom had spiraled and the responsibility was once again on my shoulders to try to get her the help that might save her life. Gossamer down was tucked under her chin, the gentle grey cotton clinging to her secret. She hid the rope burns around her neck with the comforter under which she was lying. I talked to her briefly, hugged Luke, and walked out to the garage, each step grievous with the immense gravity that held them in place. I entered the shadows of the building and moved further into the darkness, placing one wavering foot on the center of the offending stool, then the weight of the other, as I reached to pull a knife through the burlap noose that had failed her so it could be of no further use.

What's a twenty-year-old to do? I needed my mother to be okay, to be safe. She wasn't. I needed the authorities to keep my mother safe. They didn't. And I didn't have the capacity or internal strength to wrestle through what that meant in light of what I'd just witnessed. The rope, the stool, the Gossamer down. The images swirled in my brain. I needed to be safe too. I needed escape.

✶ ✶

Oakley and I went dancing, a seemingly inappropriate reaction to such a situation I thought at the time. Oakley didn't question my reasoning. She helped me move away from it, knowing the assault of this reality was too much to bear. It would find me and bludgeon my insides to a pulp, but that night I hid in the falsehood of the pulsing beat of drums and guitars and stomping feet, a favorite collegiate pastime.

The next day I had Mom recommitted—again arrested, again while Luke watched. Three weeks later, the mental institution let her go to a kind of halfway house across town from where I lived. The doctors didn't take into consideration the hoarse quivering words I spoke, the fear that showed in the trembling of my body at the thought. She was supposed to be watched there, never left alone. She would be safe, they assured me.

* *

My boyfriend, Andrew, and I stopped by her empty house a few weeks later, inhabited at the time by only the shell, the remnants, of Luke after such a trying time. Andrew wanted a desk for his apartment. I knew there was one at the house he could use. We looked inside the house and couldn't find it, then went around to the garage to see if it was in there. I found it difficult to be at home, without my mom, reminded of her absence and the reasoning behind it as I looked at the barren yard around the house.

The crunch of the snow underfoot sounded each footstep as we moved toward the garage, a footprint hollowed out for each step, an unsuspecting stride. The garage wrapped around, about thirty feet back from the front of the house. Its aged dark brown wood pressed against the now dormant lilac bushes along the drive, the door open. Back in the right-hand corner of the garage, beyond the plywood shelves, was my mom. I took a step toward her and she ever so slowly turned to barely face me, the light from the window moving from her ear to cheek to nose. What was she doing there? My reality shifted, a hitch in my consciousness. It was only when my eyes adjusted to the shadows, and my mind snaked around the twisted truth of a second glance her way, that I noticed she hadn't turned but instead was slowly swaying. The burlap rope, the noose, tormented me in slow motion until I was incensed enough to rip my gaze away.

She had left the halfway house, walked home, and hanged herself.

.... I found my mother hanging from the rafters of our garage..........

I turned around, reeling with desperation, into Andrew's arms and then pushed myself away.

"Oh my God... Oh my God... Oh my God...," I choked out, barely audible.

Do you know what 911 tells you when you first call and say you found someone who has hanged herself? They tell you to cut the person down in case she hasn't been there too long, in case you can revive her. I was paralyzed. I handed the phone to Andrew and sat on the porch with a cigarette burning itself out between my fingers, my entire body shaking as if the darkness of the situation was somehow trying to fight its way out of my body. I hunkered there until the cops came, and the coroner. I couldn't even cry. I sat and I stared blankly. My emotions were so strong within me, I felt if I let even one of them out there would be a flood and it would drown me in one breath.

.... I found my mother hanging from the rafters of our garage..........

I don't remember much of the next few months. What I vaguely do remember from that day is that a long-time friend found Luke at the mall and brought him to me so I could break the news to him. I remember planning a funeral, choosing an urn, picking out flowers, and calling all the family and friends we held dear to announce she had died. These are vague memories.

I have a mere handful of vivid memories from those days, months. I distinctly recall my dad's presence throughout. He has expressed to me that, at the time, it was hard for him to feel as though any of his actions were significant enough to ease the enormity of the suffering through which I was lumbering. I can, however, still hear the underlying notes of his presence today. The strength of his quiet melody in my heart reverberated against the walls. Just having him near me eased the burden as if he were physically sharing it.

I don't remember, specifically, what seat he claimed in my home or his placement at the funeral. I can't visualize his physical presence. Instead, I can still hear the soothing chorus of aid he provided by simply being by my side. The respite he offered still resonates within my soul, an anthem of healing my heart will forever sing.

Another distinct memory: my loyal friends. My friend and roommate, Hillary, crashed her car because she was desperately trying to get to me at my mom's house to be with me the day the cop cars and coroner van littered our street. Andrew was the only one there and she wanted to help hold me. Days later, Beth phoned, moments after speaking to her mother, to tell me she'd booked the next flight back home from Arizona and would be with me as soon as humanly possible. She shared with me in a conversation many months later that there wasn't even standing room left at the funeral.

The generosity of my mom's closest female friends as they banded together to lovingly pack up my mother's house and belongings so I didn't have to return to the place where I had endured the greatest tragedy of my life, will never be forgotten. Nor Oakley sitting on the curb with me while I waited for the hauling company to take all the boxes to a storage unit, holding my hand as we sunk down with our backs to my mom's house. She helped me sift through all the boxes months later.

Amnesia can't erase the family and friends who gathered around me and held my world together while I couldn't, picked up the fragments and cradled them gently in the sanctuary of their hearts. They gave me those things for which I was too shattered to ask and drew in around me when it took every molecule within me to merely survive.

NINETEEN

To Merely Survive

*H*ave you ever had that feeling when your world falls out from under you but there is a short period of time you feel suspended—a pause of numb weightlessness before recognition of the impending plummet to meet it? Eyes wide, looking down then back up with the understanding of a future rapid decent, face changing from fierce to fearful, and then just a puff, a hole in the middle where you hovered before, a soul you once recognized no longer in the frame?

Throughout the funeral planning and implementation, and the following days/weeks of having loved ones close, I felt numb and moved like a spectator through my own life, watched conversations, even ones I was involved in, from outside of myself. I accepted affection until overwhelmed by it and then turned to be alone. I was quiet, my heart quiet, as if paralyzed by the shock of its injuries. The pain of my loss was reflected more in the faces of those that looked upon me in empathy than in my own.

It wasn't until later that I came crashing down to meet the wreckage of my new existence. At night I would lie in bed and become overwhelmed by emotion. I would toss and turn, feeling smothered, as if grief hung in the shadows and slowly moved upon me in the night to place a pillow of agony over my face, and held it there until my body squirmed and screamed and ripped me out of bed. As I ran from my room, the shadows spilled out from the doorway and followed me down the hall, clawing at my clothes.

I would sprint into the kitchen and flip on the light to chase away the fear of suffocation. I'd stand there, trembling and choking on sadness, my cheeks feeling eroded by the force of a river of tears. Draped by the yellow of the crackling old lightbulb, I'd crawl on the couch and hold on, crying so hard no noise came from my chest as it caved in upon itself. For hours I fell apart, alone but at least sheltered from the shadows. The blanket of incandescence kept the darkness at bay.

Through the nights, waves of emotion crashed against the reality of despair, anger, guilt, compassion, shame. So many different reactions, fighting with each other, bouts waged within myself, against myself. I felt anger toward my mom and her decision. How could she have left us like that? Weren't we, her own devoted children, enough to live for? Why did she hang herself in our garage, knowing it would likely be me who found her?

My empathetic self would then become disgusted with the sucker punches I threw and step in to referee, insisting I see things more clearly from Mom's perspective. She was overcome by a terrible disease, after all, that clouded the reality of her actions. If her mind had been clear of such an emotional cancer, she would never have left us. How dare I show such rage toward someone I loved and who had been so sick?

The hardest matches were the ones I fought with guilt and shame. Guilt made known I'd done something awful. Shame laid bare the ways I'd become something awful. These were the title fights, more rounds than one could count, and never fair. Guilt was a heavyweight with years of experience under his belt. Shame an opponent with immeasurable strength. Why hadn't I done more to make sure this didn't happen? Why wasn't I enough to live for? If only I'd been there sooner. What kind of child strips her mother's dignity by having her thrown in a mental institution? What did you think would happen, you fool? Even if I could forgive her, there was no possibility of forgiving myself.

My spirit aged by decades before the dawn filtered through the blinds and I would return to my room, the T-shirt between my shoulder blades ringing with damp exhaustion and my eyes burning from salted tears. Dragged into my bed, my body would fall next to Andrew's and I'd cry again, softer tears, now coming from a different heartbreak for the fact he slept without any knowledge of my torture. Shouldn't his empathy be strong enough to rouse him out of his slumber to hold me? Couldn't he see the wounds inflicted by these bouts and step in so they didn't keep going night after night?

Every night was the same. Each morning I rose, battered and bruised with emotional black eyes and split lips tinted with hints of dried blood, to face a day among the living. I moved through my life, now a victim of my own abuse, scared and skittish, slinking only along the outskirts.

So it was for a long time. I wanted people to understand the unexplainable torture I was feeling. I reverted to an infantile set of tools to express that for which I had not developed a vocabulary. Some unsuspecting person in my midst would ask, "Are you doing OK today?" To which I would brazenly reply, "Well, I found my mom hanging from the rafters of our garage, so... it's been a time." Deadpan, no tears, just words. I'd shrug my shoulders, look the person in the eye with an apathetic expression, and be on my way to something else.

I used these outward and raw statements of my anguish to elicit validation of the tremendous energy and determination it took me to rise from my bed each morning and continue living in the skeleton of an existence I called my life. I wanted others to flinch when they imagined such a horrid scene, to feel the twist in their guts from the blow the way mine twisted. I was desperate to feel justified in the fact that I still felt broken beyond repair.

None of this behavior was calculated. In all honesty, the retelling feels like yet another betrayal, like the revealing of a dirty secret. The fact is, though, I was merely surviving. My actions were those born from the instinct to stay alive, even if just for one more breath.

The shame I still feel is unnecessary, logically. The ways by which I stumbled through such a time in my life were the only ways I knew. Reactions of this nature cannot be measured as good or bad. They're out of one's control. I've made it through twenty years now, trying to bridge the gap between logic and my heart. It's only been recently that I've rectified these two opposing parts of being, bringing them together in a friendship forged by fire. They're now more tolerant, maybe even companionable to one another, even if they can't yet fully understand their differences.

* *

As I navigated each day, whispers of reprieve arrived here and there. I'd notice an hour or two where I seemed to step out from the cloud cover and into a hint of warmth from the sunlight. It grew to possibly even a day or two of respite. On the inside it was an incredibly lonely journey. There was no one truly capable of joining such a trek. Though loved ones were always visible in my periphery, grief is near-sighted.

Even Andrew, though we shared a great love, couldn't be expected to heal me. I wanted badly for him to erase the pain. I yearned for him to do so. I looked up to him, tears washing over my childlike brown eyes, holding the shattered pieces of me out for him to take. "Please put me back together." The razor-sharp, jagged fragments would never fit the way they needed to.

I've reflected back on that relationship often. How could I have expected my boyfriend, good and solid, but also only twenty, to be able to fix me? No one can fix that kind of broken, no matter one's age or wisdom, no matter the fortitude of his love. He was dealing with his own distress of seeing a human being hanging from a noose, of witnessing the raw and unkind world at such a young age. He tried his hardest to navigate the terrain of our relationship and keep it together. He was gentle, kind, and understanding. But I had nothing to give him. I only took what he didn't have.

After six months of gradually growing apart, Andrew helped me to let go of him; he took my fingers entwined from around his and offered other's hands in hopes I could find my way back to myself. I am forever grateful for his presence then, for the way he cared for me even when that meant leaving me to my own healing. Countless times my heart has apologized to Andrew and shown him overwhelming gratitude. Maybe someday he, too, will know.

* *

Still, even now, I get jolts of the electrifying zing of remembrance. I see the rustic texture of burlap rope, watch a Western movie with Nick and a hanging scene flickers by, or a snarky teenage girl at the mall mentions flippantly that she'd rather kill herself than wear something that hideous, and a shock rushes from my spine to my spirit. I now try to sit with those feelings, even momentarily, and process the toxicity out of them. My hope in doing so is maybe one day this reaction, too, will no longer reside within me.

I purposefully share the darkness of this time because I want to honor a true portrait of myself. Painting a portrait without the use of shadows—charcoal, slate, steal blue, midnight black—depicts a flat and unnatural face, a face without the depth of laugh lines or the rounding of cheeks that accompanies a smile. I don't want to portray a lifeless, air-brushed self. Without darkness there is no light. Without despair there is no levity. Without truth the whole is not revealed.

It's because of this time in my life I can now feel equally overwhelming gratitude and love. I intentionally choose to shine a light down the cavernous pit into which I fell to illuminate a perspective, a measure of how far I've come as I stand here. I fell along the way, stumbled, scraped knuckles and knees, wanted to turn back, but continued on. My posse joined me along the trail when it was finally accessible.

Mom would have loved the posse, been delighted by Wax Night. It's unlikely she'd have claimed a seat though. I envision her making her way around the table, with tender placement of dainty hands on our shoulders, fingering our hair and hugging us just for the sheer joy of it. She would bring the wine and her always-jovial tenor and with the gold flecks in her sparkling eyes watch as the girls she helped raise grew into women. Her heart would overflow with the intimacy of us women, holding within it a deep pride. Is it possible, even, that she orchestrated Wax Night from above?

TWENTY

Mountains to Climb

*T*raversing the Rocky Mountains is not for the faint of heart. Every massif has only one summit, but to reach it you must traverse many peaks and valleys, climbing in elevation, then descending again, up-down, up-down. After Mom's departure, and before Wax Nights began, I traversed the trails of the Bridger Range and its seven major peaks that flank the eastern end of the Gallatin Valley, ultimately reaching the range's summit, Sacagawea Peak, at an elevation of 9,596 feet. I've spent much time up there, in the endeavor to "feel small," as Lynn puts it.

A climb to such a summit means a definitive departure from the familiar safety of valleys and foothills. To crest the zenith of these mountains means reaching an altitude at which trees are no longer able to survive—the tree line. The first time I encountered this microcosm, my spirit had little to show of the life that once grew below in the rich earth and sprawling green of my childhood. I felt desolate and wind-swept. Above me, however, clouds shone, not as impending storms, but as the breath of potential. They encouraged me to trudge further, exert energy forward toward the possibilities of what might be.

Nick entered my world during this ascent. His gentle soul drew me out of my sadness and relayed the difficult truth, during intimate conversations along the trail, that it was time to focus on healing. He stood before me and reached for my hands when we encountered the steepest terrain. On legs shaking with fatigue, we took long strides and finally planted our feet on the summit. His arm around my waist and my hand in the back pocket of his wranglers, we lifted our faces to the brilliance of the sun that drenched our skin in rejuvenating energy.

At these new heights, the volcanic activity of the region is made evident, showing off a large thrust fault where the continental crust buckled. The jagged tenor of 2.5-million-year-old limestone, exposed and eroded, unearthed by forces beyond comprehension, these vaulting mammoths are staggering. We looked over this landscape, held in each other's embrace. I lay my head on his chest and listened to the sound of his heart. From such a stature, the conversations came from beneath. The breath of the valleys whispered up the slopes and the piercing cry of the Bald Eagle spiraled skyward from just above the trees. Such echoes from below ushered us home.

* *

Nick and I were introduced several times along the rodeo circuit, him competing and I an onlooker smitten with the ways of the rodeo cowboys and cowgirls. I was too inexperienced in my own riding to enter the Northern Rodeo Association competitions, so I came to watch friends compete. My spirit swooned amongst the community of men and women in attendance-living history, testaments to the true grit of the West. I was often behind the chutes, watching as the men championed each other—the smell of horses' lather, the echoing sound of leather-soled boots on the wooden planked scaffolding behind the chutes, and the undertone of men's graveled voices holding one-sided negotiations with their broncs.

Nick pulled cinch ropes for other riders, distracted horses that wouldn't calm by playing with their noses, and then with his lanky arms hanging over the metal rail he studied every movement for the next eight seconds. I have a newspaper clipping taken by one of the local news reporters capturing a solitary moment before Nick's ride. In the picture he's squatting, teal and tan chaps draped over his knees, spurs touching the butt of his wranglers, black felt cowboy hat in hand, alone. His head is bowed low, fingertips pressed to his forehead; solemn, quiet, turned inward. The article is titled "Calm Before the Storm" and reads:

> Nick R. says a prayer to himself while preparing for a bronc ride at the rodeo in Helmville on Sunday. He's one of the top-ranked bareback bronc riders in the Northern Rodeo Association.

This girl wanted to ride off into the sunset with such a man, one who held a steady hand against a storm, with quiet confidence resting squarely below his hat.

It took continued effort to garner Nick's attention. Though steadfast and fearless in the arena, strapped to a bucking horse with clenched fist and his hat forced down low on his brow, he was unsteady when approached by a woman. He stood with reserve yet intrigue, etched against the backdrop of the weathered wood of the bar. A few times I sauntered across the rough-hewn dance floor, past the spotlight of the band, and asked this tall, swashbuckling man for a dance. Rarely were these propositions accepted. He was so wary of women, me in particular, that when asked to dance he would leave the bar out of fear of the unknown mystical creature that might well wrangle him and corral him for good.

In my favor was my future brother-in-law who helped keep Nick around long enough to get him 'roped.' Once I caught him, I found him more faithful and tender than any man I met before. His enduring gaze allowed me to discover the panorama of his heart. The steel blue clarity hid no secrets, told no lies, and promised he would never stray.

In this manner we traveled, side by side through mountainous terrain, building our relationship along the way. I was then invited into the loving embrace of his family. His twin sister, her husband, and their baby-to-be were the first introductions. Shortly thereafter I met his mom, Janene. Janene ushered me into her family without a second thought, bestowing endless love and pouring it over us, tendered without reservation. With hands worn from working cattle, fixing fence, and preparing meals for the men that stayed in the bunkhouse, she tended the wasteland left in my soul, brought life to that which was barren. I slowly began to flourish, the child within me once again held in the nurturing hands of a mother.

This union with Nick was different from others I shared before. The relationships of the past, fraught with continual ups and downs, passionate embraces, and equally passionate severance, seemed child's play. Nick discovered my scars and caressed them, acknowledged my strength and cherished it. He held me, placed his rough hands on the small of my back, and they encompassed the whole of it, the whole of me. A true gentleman—when embraces flushed our cheeks, he would retreat with a sigh, look over my face with consideration, and say, "I've got good brakes, too."

During our first argument, and it was a doozy, even then he proved his integrity, even while his scars blistered with whiskey. I left his house, threw myself in my truck, and slammed it in reverse. No way was I talking to him again that night.

His sister told me he called her as soon as I left:

"This better be good if you're waking me up at this hour," she said when he dialed.

"I don't know what to do. Do you and Rich ever fight? Katie just left. I really screwed up." He got quiet and she heard a beer open with a crisp crack.

She laughed before recognizing the sincere worry in his voice. "Of course, we fight. Sometimes it's not pretty. But we love each other. It'll be ok. Go to sleep. She doesn't want to talk to you tonight."

"But I don't—"

"Quit being an asshole when you drink. Call her tomorrow and apologize," she continued, then paused. "People fight, that doesn't mean they leave for good. Go to bed. I love you."

A year after we started dating, a year of the give-and-take of navigating a relationship, Nick asked me to marry him. I knew he would always be there. I trusted his commitment and love. This was the tapestry of true intimacy. For the first time in my life, I was not afraid of the future, of the unraveling. Of course, I said yes—a full-body answer that consulted my heart, my soul, my logic, my limbs. Yes!

Now I had a wedding to plan.

TWENTY-ONE

A Space in My Heart

As my husband-to-be and I navigated the months before our ceremony, my liaisons shifted guards from my girls, to Nick, and now to others. The posse was ever-present company, of course, but then entered matriarchs who would shepherd me through these momentous rites of passage. Who can plan a wedding without her mother in attendance? I yearned for Mom's energy, craved her blessing, and mourned the loss of her warmth radiating throughout the corners of our matrimony. So, I enlisted the help of the only person alive who could channel all those things: Auntie Cam.

Mom and Auntie Cam weathered storms together as they raised kids in low-income housing apartments next to each other, skinny paychecks relied on for momentum toward better lives for their families. When I asked Auntie Cam if she would companion me in Mom's absence, she confided, "There was one night, Katie," she paused and took a deep breath, "when your mom found me gripped by paralyzing pain and depression, curled up on the bathroom floor. She embraced me with nothing but tender care, drew a steaming bath, and with steady hands disrobed a kindred soul and placed me in the waters that rippled life back into the dark places." Auntie Cam's chest shook as she talked, then she rose from the chair where she was sitting and turned to gaze out the window above the sink, her voice lowering. "I can't forgive myself for not being able to save her in the same way. I can only hope to make up for it now, by loving you."

In the months to come, she painstakingly hand-sewed my wedding dress from the most luscious silk and with an intricately crafted, hand-designed and sewn corset. From a cedar chest that held some of Mom's precious fabric, Auntie Cam retrieved a square of cream "lining silk" specifically to create the innermost section of my dress. Every breath I would take on my special day would be met with a prayer, a caress from my mother. After delivering the perfect bridal gown, Auntie Cam stood up for me during the ceremony, and through sorrowful and joyful tears turned the gold-edged pages of my mother's own Bible, one thin butterfly-wing page at a time with long delicate fingers, until she came to the marked verse. She read aloud for us all, words of hope and new beginnings:

> Love is patient and kind; love does not envy or boast; it is
> not arrogant or rude. It does not insist on its own way; it is
> not irritable or resentful; it does not rejoice at wrongdoing,
> but rejoices with the truth....

As her voice carried the love of Our Father, it too rang true with the love of my mother. Nick and I stood listening as he ran his thumbs across the backs of my hands until they were nearly raw. Beth stood beside us, along with Ashley, Oakley, and others, all draped in red satin. We could hear Beth above the rest of the sniffles and occasional cough, as breath caught in her chest while she cried. The groomsmen stood in their blue jeans, scarlet vests, charcoal jackets, and felt cowboy hats. Auntie Cam continued:

> Love bears all things, believes all things, hopes all
> things, endures all things. Love never ends.... So now faith,
> hope, and love abide, these three; but the greatest of these
> is love.[1]

When the ceremony was over, hugs given, and well wishes wished, Nick and I climbed into a horse-drawn carriage and sat beaming at each other as the clip-clop of the Percheron horses' hooves carried us to the community center for the reception. Moments after entering the hall, it began to rain; the kind of rain that kisses the leaves and through which the sun still reaches

---

[1]   1 Corinthians 13:4–13

toward the earth. "I know, Mom. I love you, too," I said looking outside at the magical beauty of it all.

The reverence of the day turned to revelry. Beth jumped on stage, belted out a few songs with the band, and hours later nearly fell off of it. By then, she was down to her stocking feet—sans stockings. Dad and I danced to "Butterfly Kisses" by Tim McGraw. Harmonizing the best I was able with the country star's baritone voice, I sang into his shoulder. I adjusted his bolo tie and squeezed his arm. His muscles relaxed as we swayed.

"How'm I doin'?" he responded. "Good thing I practiced before today, huh? I'd hate to make you look bad on your big day."

From then on, we all rocked, whirled, and smirked at just-slightly embarrassing versions of our histories together, recited by those giving toasts. Luke unbuttoned his Class A uniform jacket and Matt shed his dress coat altogether.

Beth and her mom, Sarah, had to get me out of my dress before we left the community center, given the layers, lacing, and the fact that my dress had to be stitched to my corset many hours earlier. Imagine Nick attempting such an act just before we slid into the jacuzzi tub in our room. He was grateful for their effort.

Our families joined again at Sarah's house the next morning to recover and relax. The smell wafting from the oven and the rich aroma of coffee welcomed us, invited us to sit. Mimosas added a bit of celebratory zest to the late morning gathering. We savored delectable dishes: quiche and its buttery crust, fresh strawberries dripping with juices, and coffee cake with crumbly caramel on top. We were cozy, enveloped in the comfort of kinship.

"You know, Beth, you could have done a little less crying during the wedding," Sarah barbed in Beth's direction after a few rounds of conversation. "You always have to be so dramatic."

I had to choke down my sip of mimosa before bursting into laughter. "Auntie Cam was reading from Mom's Bible. Plus, Beth made up for it with her entertaining personality later."

"Yep, y'all were sure cuttin' a rug out there," she admitted.

"I couldn't move when Nick and I finally got to our room. My feet are still barely able to carry me," I added. "You were smarter than me, Ash.

Cowboy boots as part of the dress code at your wedding. Smart girl. And, they looked amazing with our dresses. I should have taken note."

"Well, I feel great," Ashley chirped.

"We know. You are... The Unicorn," Beth and I chorused.

✶ ✶

In cadence with one another, Nick and I made our way down through the foothills where the Alpine Bluegrass and Mountain Timothy waltz in the meadows. Stretching thigh high, the grasses played with my fingertips. This is where the pines and spruce congregated in audience, dressed in darker hues, tall and unwavering with their heavier constitutions. Further into the bottoms, the foliage was vibrant with splashes of lime from the fresh aspen leaves in contrast with the chalk and chestnut of its bark. Flowers burst with the energy of burnt umber, periwinkle, and sunshine. We weaved through the quaking aspens and cottonwood trees that embraced the river bottoms, my senses filled with the smell of lush moss and ferns, whirled by the air that skipped above the gurgling water. There we paused to merely enjoy the journey, and to find each other.

✶ ✶

Three years later, Janene—Nick's mom—was there for me when we had our first baby. She lived with us when JD was born, and for the first five years of his life. She was a blessing. Through watching her with JD, I was able to learn the ways of motherhood. She taught me things any new mom needs to know, not by telling me what I was doing wrong. Instead, she draped JD over her knee and bounced him gently while rubbing his back in a circle to get his tummy to feel better. She supported his head with the placement of a palm on his chest, his chin cupped by her fingers, as only a seasoned mother would. Bathing him in the sink, bringing water over his head with the cups of her hands, washing each tiny finger and toe, she would hum a song that bridged their hearts.

She sourced from the toolbox equipped throughout her many years of cherishing and raising her own children. I was encouraged to snuggle JD close to my chest when all I wanted to do was walk away from him. She'd come out of her room when I was up with his screaming, tiny self for the tenth time during the night and sit on the couch and be with me. She didn't take him from me, didn't tell me the ways I could make it better if I would just rub his back instead of bouncing him incessantly around the living room. She just sat with me, a blanket draped over her legs, running her arthritic fingers through the ties on the sides of the pillows.

These are the ways the knowledge and spirits of our ancestors are translated to the souls of new generations. As a chieftainess would hold the hands of indigenous women at the top of the peaks to celebrate transitions of life, so did Auntie Cam and Janene celebrate our union in marriage. As native mothers brought forth striking babies with full heads of black hair and futures pouring from within their dark, pooled eyes into their tribes, so did the matriarchs in my life. With such support in my life, from these remarkable women, I rose from the ashes.

It is with the utmost humility I say I am only afforded this good fortune because I lost my mom. The enormity of the void Mom left allowed a space in my heart big enough to let these other women in. One of my life's greatest losses gained me astonishing blessings. During mountainous climbs alone and with my cherished cowboy, both the clarity and intensity of the peaks and the tranquility and contentment of the valleys offer solace. Matriarchs have guided me through the momentous transitions of my life. My posse, however, rides with me always. And on occasion, we ride bareback.

TWENTY-TWO

Full Moon on a Hot Night

After sharing the exposed, tender, and naked emotions of our lives, it is only appropriate that we're able to balance these by sharing raw and unclad encounters of the playful kind. With the ability to go to the depths of despair, in kind we are offered the gift of sharing depths of hilarity—the pendulum soars equally in both directions.

As mothers and professionals, we keep ourselves put together the majority of the time. These nights together, without airs, allow us to abandon the confines of our jobs, our families, and our clothes. Even though this kind of interaction may seem foreign when compared to the longstanding representation of an auspicious housewife—the picture of women descending from the pilgrims—this might actually be the closest we come to honoring the global depictions of historical clans' women. This time together has become the backbone of our friendships.

＊ ＊

With Christmas approaching, our schedules will soon fill with family gatherings, holiday soirees, and the like. Tonight, we gather for our last Wax Night of the year. Beth and I walk into Lynn's house for this session, seeing that Kenzie and Jax have already arrived. I can hear Jax's voice before I turn the corner to the living room, "Work's been dreadful. I barely have time to breathe these days." The three of them are sitting at the kitchen table. Beth puts her beer in the fridge, and we give hugs around.

Vintage holiday music dances in the background as we exchange hugs and conversations. There are three bottles of champagne on the counter by several wine glasses, and choices of orange, grapefruit, and pomegranate juices to mix everyone's favorite mimosas. The sunset colors draw our eyes. Such fancy beverages are Lynn's and Jax's preferred way to ring in the holidays. They provided the libations tonight.

We all congregate at the counter to unite champagne and juice in our favor. The jingle of charms on each of our glass stems is one of my favorite sounds. The peach champagne and pomegranate juice bring sweetness to the party as they do my palate. My attention now turns to the table, where a platter of meats and cheeses currently resides. Jax notices the excitement spreading across my face as my eyes wander over the offering.

"Do you like my charcuterie board? I personally penned each of those name flags."

"I do. Your calligraphy is impeccable. It all looks delicious. So, what do we have here?" I ask as I gander at the indicators, drawn in wistful flourish.

Genoa salami, smoked gouda, prosciutto, horseradish cheddar, chorizo, dill Havarti, serrano ham, and Merlot BellaVitano, all cheerfully identified. Baguette bread slices, cut on an angle, border the edges, and in the middle of the board a dish overflows with all hues of olives, big and small, stuffed and pitted. Not to be outdone by the savory items, to the right is displayed a delicate teal serving dish with a divine assembly of homemade sweet chili jam, chili dark chocolate shards, and sea salt caramels.

Ashley dances in through the door and around the corner, cradling two bottles of wine. In perfect counterpoint to the fancy table spread, she has her Carhartt work pants on, hammer loop and carpenter pockets included. She's covered in a multitude of paint colors, some of which are flecked in her hair. It appears this might be the first break of her entire day.

"Sorry I'm late, girls. I had to finish that remodel we're doing. I decided to just do it myself. Anyway, I'm here now and ready to pop the corks on these beauties." She looks at the bottles with longing and then cruises toward the laden table.

We settle ourselves after choosing from the platters and transition into mature conversation. "I just want you all to know I went shopping yesterday," I chime in. "I know it's hard to believe, given what a thrill I get from the mind-numbing exercise, but it's true. Ashley and I went. And, I have a public service announcement. Please listen closely: I highly recommend that you don't take Ashley to shop for bras. She has no legitimate context with which to judge the fit for anyone who actually has boobs." This garners smirks and nods in recognition of a statement of truth. Ashley has no filter for her facial expressions and glares at me over her wine glass.

"So, we were in the dressing room and I was trying on all different types." I pop a cheese-stuffed olive in my mouth and chew. "Why do bras have to be hard to fit? You'd think the lingerie gods would have figured this out by now. Anyway, I found one I actually thought was equipped and sized fairly well." I pause for dramatic levity.

"Do you know what Ashley asked in her wonder-what-it-feels-like-to-have-boobs naivete? She brushed across my shoulders to grasp the front and top of the straps with her fingers, pulled them up about three inches, looked me straight in the eye and asked, 'Don't you want them up here?'" I lift my shirt to demonstrate accordingly as I share.

Everyone in this group is wealthily endowed, except Ashley. She is one of those ever-so-lucky women who can get away with *nada* and no one's the wiser.

I continue, "To which I responded, 'Of course I want them up there! Unfortunately, honey, that's not how gravity works.'"

Ashley laughs and throws her own shirt up in response—not even a little sport bra is to be found. "Girls, this is what I have to work with. Nothing. You can't deny that I have little to base such questioning on."

"Seriously," Jax says, cupping her own overflowing bosom, "there's no brassiere in this world that can bring these babies back 'up here.'"

Every woman I know has boobs; most have stretchmarks and some are etched with cesarean scars. We're women with storied bodies that God made and not afraid to bare them in the company of women we love and trust. God made these beautiful conduits for our souls and was masterful in doing so.

We do have a rule that this is not a show-and-tell opportunity, though. What happens at Wax Night, stays at Wax Night. That is, until I get everyone's permission and it's published for all the world to read....

Lynn glides over to Ashley and gives an enduring hug, pulls her paint-splashed T-shirt tighter around her chest, and winks in our direction. She gets back to the task at hand and asks Ashley, "Are you waxing tonight? I might need to cut more strips if you are. I figured I'd ask. And, Katie, take of your pants. You're up."

"No, I think I might be done waxing," Ashley responds. "I always get ingrown hairs when I wax, and I don't when I shave. Besides, you all have witnessed that I just have too much hair. I tried laser hair removal, even. I tried it for months and months. Apparently, it doesn't work on everyone, because I endured the torture with lackluster results. I've accepted my fate and now just shave it all. I leave nothing. It works out."

Kenzie shakes her head as Ashley says this, and crinkles her nose. "I don't wax because I'm not going to take my clothes off—ever—in front of all you bitches, and because it doesn't work for me either. I might as well have been from the Amazon. I just let it grow."

Jax takes a long drink, then paints a picture with her words, "I can just see your husband now, Kenz. You're in the bedroom for sexy time and he throws on his safari hat, unbuttoned khaki shirt, and camo boxers. He eagerly embarks, pushing his way deeper into the wild and untamed bush." This visual has me giggling, and the rest join as they picture it.

"Ack, stop!" Kenzie counters, laughing, with a slightly pink hue to her cheeks.

"Rod doesn't care, really," Beth chimes in. "He's happy to play no matter what the terrain. Not like The Ass I was married to before. I just do what I want for myself and he's more than happy to enjoy the results."

Well played.

We all take a break to have a few sips, mine from a straw as I lie in position between the island and cupboards of the kitchen. Beth continues, "You know what else I can do now that I'm not married to The Ass?"

"Rod!" retorts Kenzie.

This garners a raucous outburst. Jax ends up with her drink up her nose, which makes the rest of us nearly pee our pants (yep, all with pants on–other than myself–currently getting my own jungle landscaped).

"Oh my God! Stop," Beth says. "I was going to say I can now yawn! Every time I yawned when I was with The Ass, he would stick his finger in my mouth to be obnoxious." Beth is still hardly able to compose herself.

"Nick likes about this much left to play with," I say, drawing a line around the landing strip on my partially bare self. The girls nod in acknowledgement. "But he knows a routine of a clean-shaven face is the way I like it on him. Anytime he chooses to comment on his excitement for Wax Night treatment, I take the opportunity to comment on his state of tidiness. All's fair."

"Does anyone else know what a merkin is?" I say, shifting positions and topics.

"No," they harmonize.

I start laughing before I can get out any words. The girls will eat this up. "A merkin, friends, is a little toupee for your coochee. It was a way for women to still have hair down there, if they wanted, even after they waxed it all off for sanitary reasons. Kate Winslet wore one for her role in *The Reader* because she waxed for years before. It was set during WWII when women were rustic, I guess."

"Are you kidding me?" Kenzie asks, astonished. "Now I have to watch that movie, for one. And, who thinks this shit up?"

"That's the best thing I've ever heard," Beth sings. "Like a fake mustache for your vagina? Oh, that's gold."

"Better hope it doesn't wander during coitus. That'd be a new sort of embarrassing," Jax adds. "Not quite sure how that actually works, practically."

"So, Jax," I question. "Speaking of coitus... How's it going with the Italian Stallion? Any embarrassing stories you should share with us on that front?"

"Nah," Jax replies with a shrug. "I was too much of a woman for him to handle." She gets up and moves to the counter for a refill of champagne. "Our conversations just kind of faded. I think he may have even gained a girlfriend now. We still visit now and then, but he was all hat and no cattle."

"Well, I guess you didn't get to clear the cobwebs after all," Beth interjects. "But it was fun while it lasted."

"True. Between the conversations and pictures and heavy petting, it was worth the investment of time," Jax concurs.

Mm-hm, women are allowed to talk about sex, too, you know. We don't delve into raunchy and dirty detail, don't give away our lover's secrets or betray their trust. We are full of love to share with committed partners who make us feel sexy and whole. No hot-dish housewives here, with pallor on their faces. We embrace all aspects of our lives, talk about sex, and bare our naked selves on occasion, just as we are then able to bare the grief and pain of our hardest situations.

∗ ∗

In retrospect, I guess Wax Night is like a marinade of gratitude which brings a tenderness and sweetness to this heart that might otherwise be left tough and bitter. Take one already leathered heart, throw it on the embers of a mother's death by her own hand, and you come away with something no one could stomach. Take that same leathered heart, however, pour over it a mixture of five parts friendship, two parts sweet and savory sons, one part loving man, and rub with a generous seasoning of family. Allow to marinate in the gratitude of these ingredients as long as possible, and you have the perfect recipe to bring a heart to its most tender and yielding glory.

My friends, my mentors, my mothers have provided me a lifetime supply of such nourishment. There's no better way to count my blessing at the end of each year than to share an evening with those closest to me. The posse gathers around the table each winter, just as we do tonight. We carry on in this fashion for hours, sharing nourishing food and refreshing drinks. As things are winding down, we raise our glasses in a toast.

"To the greatest friends on the planet," Beth croons. "Where would we be without each other?"

"To us," we chime in, clink glasses, and drink together one last time for this year. We put our glasses down, and with a giggle I toss a pillow across the living room, messing Jax's hair with the effort.

"What in the hell was that for?" she exclaims, scowling in my direction.

"Couldn't have a party without a pillow fight, now could we?"

Afterword

We part for the evening, sharing hugs all around, and I meander home. I enter the front door and the full moon peeks from around the silhouetted mountains, reaches through the kitchen window, and I'm blanketed by its full weight. Weaving through the rooms of our home on my way to bed, I savor the quiet moment lit by the Christmas lights. I linger in our living room and gaze at the large framed photograph of sleek horses running through water, then turn toward the boys' rooms. I creak open JD's door, make my way to his lamp-lit bed, and kiss him on the forehead.

"Goodnight, Baby."

"One more chapter? Please."

"Alright. But you need your sleep," I pause and enjoy his innocent gaze below sweeping lashes. "Love you, kiddo."

"Love you, too."

Seven steps down the hall, I tiptoe to Sammy's bedside. He's stretched out, half uncovered, revealing his bare chest. How's my baby already so big? Leaning down to kiss his shoulder, I allow myself to stay a moment longer to memorize him. Unable to yet pull myself out from under his spell, my cheek rests upon his chest lightly. There I linger until we both exhale.

"Goodnight, Baby," I whisper as my spirit swoons.

"I wish you could meet these boys, Mom. I know you would have laughed with them, danced with them, and held them close. Today was a near-perfect day. I hope you're up there, somewhere, sharing it with me."

Entering my room, I fall into my down comforter wearing a heart swollen with love and pride, making my dreams almost indistinguishable from the reality of my day. Nick, sound asleep, reaches over and pulls my body closer. I place my hand on his chest and drift off.

⁂　⁂

Despite all the dark and painful things I've shared herein, here I am, a person who's filled with joy and compassion. I'm a strong woman, not just for myself but also for my family and friends, many of whom you've met in these pages. I am whole (enough), I'm remarkable just the way I am, and still growing... as you are too.

Thank you for holding my hand and walking beside me as I put these hardships, tales, these women, this love into words. Throughout this journey, I've shared with you the truths I hold dear, about the women who occupy my heart, and the friendships that bring light to even the darkest places. I bared myself to you, shared with you my most brilliant moments and deepest despair. I've stripped away pleasantries and revealed the primal essence of what makes us human, what makes us women, and what allows you and I to truly connect.

I share my story as an offering, an offering of hope you can hold while embracing women in your life and banding together to enjoy connections of your own. It's my desire that the camaraderie you and I have built will illuminate the road you travel from here, spilling forth before you.

In the countless words I've written, and rewritten and burned and saved, I've still not adequately described what a blessing true depth of friendship can be. I've called upon my posse many times over, and I know I need them just as much now as in the past. Storms come over us all, sometimes when the forecast is sunshine. To have women around me whom I can count on when my next storm hits is a gift I can only repay by offering the same.

Bringing each remarkably different personality and background, the posse has ebbed and flowed throughout years of separation and transition, sometimes moving forward, sometimes getting caught in the eddies of bad choices. The tides still pull us this way and that with the waxing and waning of the moon. The way we learn, grow, and build upon these lessons enables us to be the fullest versions of ourselves upon our return. Having a community willing and able to walk us through the momentous changes in our lives, to bring ceremony to the rites of passage we all make our ways through, brings a value that cannot be measured.

For these reasons I encourage you to leave these pages, dear one, and allow yourself to do the terrifying—dare to try again until you truly, deeply connect with trustworthy women in your life.

On a soapbox side note... I don't consider social media to be honest or true connections with my friends. Texts really don't offer a depth of intimacy either. I have to get face to face and heart to heart with those people I value. Never will technology afford me the empathy glistening in a friend's eyes. A meme won't make me laugh as hard as a reminiscent phone conversation with an old friend. Online comments don't adequately convey a friend's beaming pride for one of my accomplishments. Some of the loneliest women I know have thousands of online friends and nothing in their hearts to show for it. These avenues of flimsy associations will never impact a heart in the way true interaction can. It takes being right by one another's side, physically and in real time whenever possible, to support each other.

I implore you, make the effort to deliberately create valuable interactions with local friends. Confide in them your secrets and trust they will cherish the opportunity. Allow them to see your vulnerability and receive the gift of being able to do the same in return. Forgive when they cannot forgive themselves and find respite and rejuvenation in their company, their arms. Schedule your own interpretation of Wax Night, a regular invitation for companionship, and see what grows from the effort. It will be beautiful. Not perfect, but beautiful.

FROM THE PAGES OF BOOK TWO IN THIS
SERIES:
Raising Pups in Montana:
The Strength We Discover in Ourselves as Mothers,
and Howling Adventures of the Pack

Parenting Advice

You think having a wax strip yanked off your upper lip or nether region is rough? You should try navigating the road of receiving parenting advice from your well-meaning friends, who also happen to know you and all your vices and weak spots. This offering of opinion has a "No Trespassing" sign hung on the barbed-wire fence. The only access to this expansive pasture is by the winding back roads, with their deep borrow ditches and washboards—roads often traveled alone.

When it comes to parenting, sharing one's opinion is hard because we feel the most insecure and therefore most defensive about our rearing efforts. Offering a counterpoint to someone's decision as a parent is often not taken as advice, but instead as an affront to their dedication to their children. We women in the posse tenuously walk this line together. We join the ranks of all mothers who've questioned decisions they've made. Where's the guidebook, the bible for parenting tips? Doesn't parenting without a guidebook mean we would be more open to other resources?

⋆ ⋆

I'm so desperate for help during our Wax Night together, I would receive— with open arms even—an invitation from Cruella de Vil if she offered support. Maybe her ideas weren't all that terrible? I'm struggling with my youngest during bedtime. It has devoured my energy in a multitude of unsavory bites. Sammy has such a strong will and, though I'm certain it will serve him in his future endeavors, it's not serving anyone when it comes to getting his tired three-year-old butt to bed.

At this juncture, in our girls' night, it's both my turn to wax and my turn to share.

"OK, Katie. Take off your pants. I'm done with my turn for torture," Beth says as she gingerly wiggles into her red and black plaid lumberjack-looking leggings and clears the way. We never tire of directing one another to take off her pants, especially if they are hideous leggings. It has a certain ring to it, and we all try to employ it whenever possible. "Good luck down there!"

I sashay my way past my trusted girls and assume the position. As I'm arranging the couch pillow purposefully under my head, I start in about my frustration, "I can't believe how stubborn this kid is. I'm trying my best to just hold out one more time than he does. He just won't give up. I put him to bed the other night. He got back out of bed. So, I put him back in bed and he started screaming and got back out.

"I made one last clutch effort this week; I'd be the better person. I am his mother and I would win. I'd put him back in bed calmly, without saying a word, each time he got out. My hope was that he'd tire of this battle and succumb. The first night I put him back in bed twenty-five times. I don't know why, but somehow counting the times was reaffirming... like I'd been strong and calm twenty-five times."

"Counting twenty-five times of putting him back in bed, for me, would not be calming. I'd lose my shit," Kenzie states as fact. The other girls nod in agreement.

"Well, that lost its luster after the first five minutes, or round eight." I place both my hands on my temples and rub my eyes intensely. Although the conversation thus far has been lighthearted, tears from exhaustion now fill the corners of my eyes and run down into my ears. I raise my voice in frustration, "I put that little puke back in bed seventy-six times last night. Seventy-six damn times he got back out of his bed after I'd put him in it. I. Don't. Know. What. To. Do. He's impossible." I throw an arm over my face. I'm beyond discouraged.

"That has to be so infuriating. I don't know. Have you tried lying down with him?" Lynn responds in her calm and soothing way, gently placing a hand on my knee.

"I have, but then he won't fall asleep. He won't quit talking to me. He never quits talking. Talks in his sleep, even. Not that I've been able to witness that lately. Besides, what will I do then? How will I be able to get him out of that routine?" I say in earnest. This sounded like a trap he would set for me. You give this kid an inch and he heads to Hawaii.

For updates and publication information for Book Two, *Raising Pups in Montana: The Strength We Discover in Ourselves as Mothers, and Howling Adventures of the Pack*, check out katiedawnbooks.com.

About the Author

Katie Dawn is a native-born Montana author who rejoices in the beauty of deep crimson sunsets reflecting off the snow-capped Rocky Mountains, and breathing in the unmistakable essence of a horse's lather.

Being raised in small-town Montana forged both hardship and joy in abundance and allowed a vibrant backdrop for earning her English degree at MSU. Although literature classes battered her with the workload, creative writing courses danced new life throughout her spirit and set her sights on putting paper to pen to scribe depictions of all that she's made of.

In her memoir series, blog, and short essays, she writes with a raw authenticity that engages the irreverent and sacred potential of femininity, balanced by a depth of vulnerability that truly resonates throughout a reader's soul. Such written meanderings have healed broken places within her own heart and those of her readers.

The depth of character with which she writes about hardship is met by an equal measure of sharp wit and hilarity. Her ability to elevate a reader to new heights on both ends of the pendulum is spectacular.

Her most tenacious love is shown toward her husband, the two boys they ushered into the world, her family, and a sisterhood of close friends.

Should you be out in Montana and pass her by, tip your hat with a smile. Or, connect with her at katiedawnbooks.com.